ST. JOSEPH
OF COPERTINO

ST. JOSEPH
OF COPERTINO

THE REV. ANGELO PASTROVICCHI, O.M.C.

ENGLISHED AND ADAPTED

BY

THE REV. FRANCIS S. LAING, O.M.CAP.

WITH SIX ILLUSTRATIONS

TAN BOOKS AND PUBLISHERS, INC.
Rockford, Illinois 61105

NIHIL OBSTAT

Fr. Aloysius, O. M. Cap.
Fr. Felix M., O. M. Cap.
Censores Deputati.

IMPRIMATUR

Fr. Ignatius, O. M. Cap.
Minister Provincialis.

NIHIL OBSTAT

Sti. Ludovici, die 27 Aprilis, 1918

F. G. Holweck,
Censor Librorum.

IMPRIMATUR

Sti. Ludovici, die 29 Aprilis, 1918

✠*Joannes J. Glennon,*
Archiepiscopus,
Sti. Ludovici.

TAN BOOKS AND PUBLISHERS, INC.
P. O. Box 424
Rockford, Illinois 61105

1980

CONTENTS

CONTENTS

MARIAE IMMACULATAE,

"REGINAE ORDINIS MINORUM"
(Pius X, Sept. 8, 1910)

"MATRI BONORUM STUDIORUM"
(Pius X, May 16, 1906)

ECSTATIC FLIGHT OF ST. JOSEPH OF
COPERTINO

In presence of the Princess of Savoy. The Princess
wears the habit of a Tertiary

From an old print

LIST OF ILLUSTRATIONS

PREFACE

" Some persons derive most benefit from reading the Lives of the Saints in which the supernatural and the extraordinary abound. They delight to see the wonderful display of the power of Divine grace in so frail a creature as man. These biographies, that are written more for our admiration than for our imitation, strengthen our faith in the supernatural, and inspire us with a great confidence in the goodness and power of God. And certainly in these days we need to stimulate and strengthen the life of faith and trust in Providence." [1]

The rapturous flights of St. Joseph of Copertino have hardly a parallel as to frequency and duration in the lives of the saints. What is related of Christina Mirabilis, who lived 1150-1224, has been suspected of exaggeration,[2] but our

[1] Cardinal Vaughan, The Young Priest, London, 1904, p. 108.

[2] A. Kaufmann, Thomas von Chantimpré, Cologne, 1899, pp. 41-43.

saint, "having lived in more recent times, this his miraculous characteristic could easily be established in an authentic manner." [3]

Father Pastrovicchi wrote his life of St. Joseph on the occasion of the beatification of the saint,

[3] J. Görres, Die christliche Mystik, Regensburg, vol. II, p. 539.— Daumer, a one-time bitter enemy of Christianity, regards these miraculous facts as well established by reason of the "mistrust and suspicion to which St. Joseph was subject during life . . . and the severity with which the ecclesiastical enquiry concerning him was conducted." Apropos of Fr. Pastrovicchi's biography he writes: "It appears to be in keeping with fairness and the general rules of historical criticism to accept the results of such an investigation." (Christina Mirabilis, etc., pp. 7, 38).— Note the following words of Norman Douglas, a Protestant, in the *North American Review* (vol. CXCVIII, July, 1913, pp. 100–107: A Pioneer of Aviation): ". . . it may be urged that a kind of enthusiasm for their distinguished brother monk may have tempted the inmates of his convent to exaggerate his rare gifts. Nothing of the kind. He performed flights not only in Copertino, but in various large towns of Italy, such as Naples, Rome, and Assisi. And the spectators were by no means an assemblage of ignorant personages, but men whose rank and credibility would have weight in any section of society" (p. 103). For the rest, this article of Mr. Douglas is, at best, but a cynical travesty. The author repeats this "trace of light fooling," as he styles it (p. 160), with additions, decidedly stupid and scurrile, in Old Calabria, Boston, 1915, pp. 68–79. He quotes the edition of Pastrovicchi published in 1767, which he terms the "official biography." The dedication by Father Rossi misled him to regard Fr. Rossi as the author.

1753. Pope Benedict XIV, to whom the work is dedicated, wished that for each fact related the episcopal and apostolic processes should be cited. This was done. Father Suyskens remarks that the caution of citing the official documents was well employed. " Since the words of the Psalmist, ' God is wonderful in His saints ' (Ps. 67, 36), were verified in a singular manner in the life of St. Joseph, it was fitting that the extraordinary facts of his life should be attested in such a manner that credence could not be denied them." [4]

Father Gattari regards these miracles [5] as wrought in support of the doctrine of the Real Presence, the authority of the Pope, sacramental Confession and the veneration due to saints,

---

[4] Acta Sanctorum, September, tom. V, p. 993.

[5] On the supernatural character of rapturous flights see the discussion, "Is There a Natural Levitation?" in The Graces of Interior Prayer, by A. Poulain, S. J., London, 1912, pp. 550–554; Surbled-Sleumer, Die Moral in ihren Beziehungen zur Medizin und Hygiene, II (Hildesheim, 1909), pp. 174–181. " The Church has certainly not based canonization on the single fact of levitation, but without doubt she regards it as the hand of God. She looks to the habits of life of the favored person, and in particular to the circumstances of the levitation itself for proof of the supernatural character of this repeated phenomenon " (pp. 178–9).

truths which in the time of the saint were impugned by the followers of Luther and other heretics. The fame of the flights of St. Joseph spread throughout Europe and led to conversions as in the case of the Duke of Brunswick.[6] Another explanation offered is, that these miracles counteracted the diabolical arts (witchcraft and necromancy, especially in the kingdom of Naples) and superstition then prevalent.[7]

To a degree our biography is a " panegyric," with its drawbacks of " generalization " and " superlatives," but it is by no means " a dreary inventory of virtues and miracles." Some of the narratives, as in Chapter VI and IX, are very charming, " invested with all that tender simplicity and charm . . . which voiced itself in the poetic narratives of the Fioretti."

This first extensive biography of St. Joseph of Copertino in English was made from Sintzel's German translation of Fr. Pastrovicchi's Life of the saint. Only after years was it possible to procure the Italian original and verify the rendering. In the editions of Pastrovicchi of 1753 and 1767 the text is not divided into chapters; these

[6] Gattari, Prefazione.
[7] Gattari, 1. c., Montanari, pp. XIV–XV.

(thirty in all) are indicated by Roman numerals
at the beginning of paragraphs; the chapter titles
and the references to the Acts are printed in the
margin. The division of the text and the chapter
titles in the present work are new. The original
marginal titles are preserved in part as sub-titles
in the Table of Contents. The numerous references to the Acts in the original have been
omitted; likewise, in the interest of delicacy or
conciseness, several passages in the body of the
work. Details of the canonization,[8] sanctuary,
etc., have been added. Other small additions
have been made throughout the work, dates and
names have been inserted, and obscure passages
made clear. The editions used for these changes
are marked in the bibliographical list.

Many friends have aided in preparing this little book. The Conventual Fathers at Osimo
kindly donated a copy of the first edition of
Pastrovicchi. During a visit to Rome Rev.
A. T. Ennis (Concordia, Kansas) procured for
me several rare works. Some of the bibliograph-

---

[8] Chapter 30 differs in the editions of 1753 and 1767, the
latter edition substituting an account of the three miracles
approved in the process of canonization for that of thirteen miracles in the earlier edition and omitting the documents (pp. 97–108) of the first edition.

ical details I owe to Rev. Edward Jannitto, O. M. C. (Osimo), Rev. Michael Bihl, O. F. M. (Quaracchi), Rev Fr. Maurice, O. M. Cap. (Quebec), and Rev Engelbert Rosenmaier, O. M. Cap. (Milwaukee). All these I sincerely thank, as, too, the Franciscan Fathers (Washington) and the Benedictine Fathers (Atchison) for the use of books, Rev. Felix M. Kirsch, O. M. Cap. (Herman, Pa.) and other fellow-religious for suggestions toward improving the manuscript.

F. S. L.

BIBLIOGRAPHY

(Pages not numbered are given in (). The editions marked by * were used in preparing the present translation.)

"The only copy in Italy of the Acta Beatificationis et Canonizationis of St. Joseph of Copertino is that of the Congregation of Rites. The copy belonging to our Order [Conventuals] is now in the National Library at Paris, whither it was taken by Napoleon I. We [Conventuals at Osimo] have a copy of the Summario, published at Rome, Typis Reverendae Camerae Apostolicae, 1688." (Rev. Edward G. M. Iannitto, Librarian and Archivist of the Sanctuary of St. Joseph of Copertino at Osimo.)

Beatificationis et canonizationis Josephi a Cupertino Ord. Min. nova positio super dubio an, et de quibus miraculis constet in casu et ad effectum de quo agitur, Romae, 1751, 125 pp. fol°.

*Summarium additionale novae respons. super eodem dubio, Romae, 1751, 74 pp. fol°. * Positio super dubio an et de quibus miraculis constet in casu. . . . Romae, Typ. Cam. Apost., 1764. 37, 160, 17, 63, 48 pp. fol°.*

Positio noviss. super dubio an et de quibus miraculis constet in casu, et ad effectum de quo agitur, Romae, 1766, fol°.

Relazione della solenne Canonizzazione dei Beati Giovanni Canzio, G. Calasanzio, GIUSEPPE da COPERTINO, G. Emiliani, Serafino da Monte

Granaro detto d'Ascoli, Giovanna Francesca Fremiot de Chantal, celebrata . . . dalla Santita di N. S. Clemente XIII . . . il di 16 Luglio, 1767 . . . Romae, 1767, 4°.

Mariotti, Josephus Andreas, *Acta Canonizationis sanctorum Johannis Cantii, Josephi Calasanctii. . . . JOSEPHI a CUPERTINO, Hieronymi Aemiliani, Seraphini ab Asculo et Johannae Franciscae Fremiot una cum apostolicis litteris. . . . Clementis XIII. Collecta ac Notationibus illustrata a J. A. Mariotti, fidei subpromotore, Romae, 1769, fol°.*

Nuti, Roberto, O. M. C., *Vita del servo di Dio P. Giuseppe da Copertino, Palermo, 1678; Vienna, Viviani, 1682.* "This book was translated into Latin and Bohemian, *Vita servi Dei Josephi de Copertino . . . in latinum translata per* P. Marianum Unczovsky, *Pragae.* From this is taken (with omissions) *Lebensbeschreibung des grossen Dieners Gottes Joseph von Copertino . . . Brünn, 1695.*" (Daumer, p. 37, note.)

Bernino, Domenico, *Vita del Padre Fr. Giuseppe da Copertino de' Minori Conventuali . . . dedicata al . . . Innocenzo XIII, * Roma, Tinassi & Mainardi, 1722, (XVIII), 544, (XII). pp. 4°; Venezia, 1724, 4°; Venezia, 1739, 4°; Venezia, 1753, 4°; Roma, 1767; Venezia, 1768, 8°.*

——, *Vie de St. Joseph de Cupertino de l'Ordre des Frères Mineurs Conventuels, Paris, Poussielgue, 1856; Paris-Auteuil, Oeuvre de la première communion et des Orphelins apprentis, 1899.* Parts of the original, e. g., ch. VIII and XXX, are omitted, other parts are abbreviated in this translation.

Bernino is followed by Léon de Clary, O. F. M., *L'aureole seraphique, vie des Saints et des Bienheureux des trois Ordres de St. Francois, vol. III (Paris, 1882), pp. 439–460;*— Italian translation by Marino Marcucci, O.F.M., *L'Aureola Serafica, vol. III (Quaracchi, 1899), pp. 455–477;*— English translation, *Lives of the Saints and Blessed of the Three Orders of St. Francis, vol. III (Taunton, 1885), pp. 205–221.*

Agelli, Paolo Antonio, O. M. C., *Vita del Beato Giuseppe di Copertino dell' Ordine de' Minori Conventuali di S. Francesco dedicata all' Altezza Serenissima di Giuseppe Arciduca D'Austria, Venezia, Recurti, 1753.*

Pastrovicchi, Angelo, O. M. C., *Compendio della vita, virtù e miracoli del B. Giuseppe di Copertino . . . dedicata al . . . Benedetto XIV., * Roma, Zempel, 1753 (XII), 108, pp. 4°; * Roma, Zempel, 1767, XX, 119, pp. 4°* (Dedicated to Clement XIII by Fr. Dominic Rossi; Pastrovicchi's name does not appear on the title-page); *Osimo, 1804, 8°.*

*——, Latin translation by Constantine Suyskens, S. J., in *Acta Sanctorum, September, tom. V, Paris, Palme, 1868, pp. 1015–1047.*

——, *Saint Joseph de Copertino . . . Abrégé de sa vie. . . . Traduction de* M. Denis, *revue par* M. Viguier. *Avec des additions considerables, Paris, 1820, XLVIII, 280 pp. 12°.*

*——, *Leben des hl. Joseph von Copertino . . . übersetzt von* Michael Sintzel *und einem seiner Freunde, Augsburg, Rieger, 1843 (VIII), 100 pp. 8°.*

Pastrovicchi, Angelo, O. M. C., *Das tugend- und wundervolle Leben des hl. Joseph von Copertino, von einem katholischen Priester, Aachen, Cramer, 228 pp. 18°*. This reproduces the earliest German translation of Pastrovicchi's work, published at Coeln, 1753, 2nd ed. 1768, with changes in the arrangement of matter.

*——, *Compendio della vita del beato Giuseppe da Copertino, estratto della vita stampata in Roma e dedicata al . . . Benedetto XIV.* [= Pastrovicchi], *Verona, Andreoni, 1753, 32 pp. 8°*.

* Suyskenus, Constantinus, S. J., *Acta Sanctorum, September, tom. V, pp. 992–1014*. Biography, for which Bernino, Agelli and Pastrovicchi were used. The *Acta Sanctorum* were followed by Butler, *Lives of the Saints, September, 18*, and Donin, *Leben und Thaten der Heiligen Gottes, V.³, Graz, Styria, 1880, pp. 226–232*, and they are the chief source of Stadler, *Heiligen-Lexikon, vol. III, Augsburg, Schmid, 1869, pp. 461–464*.

Compendium vitae, virtutum et miraculorum necnon actorum in causa canonizationis S. Josephi a Copertino, professi Ord. Min. S. Francisci Conventualium, Romae, 1767, 28 pp. 4°.

* Montanari, Gius. Ignazio, *Vita e Miracoli di San Giuseppe da Copertino, Fermo, Paccasassi, 1851, XVI, 587, LXXIX pp. 4°*.

* Daumer, G. F., *Christina Mirabilis, das Wundergeschöpf des 12. Jahrhunderts und der hl. Joseph von Copertino, der Wundermann des 17. Jahrhunderts, Paderborn, Junfermann, 1864, 102 pp. 32°*. Follows Nuti, *Palermo, 1678;* pp. 29–102 are devoted to St. Joseph.

* Gattari, Filippo, O. M. C., *Vita di S. Giuseppe da Copertino, Osimo, Rossi, 1898 (VIII), 177 pp. 8°.*

Nine autograph letters of St. Joseph of Copertino are preserved in the sanctuary at Osimo; others are preserved at Assisi, Padua, Recanati, Rieti and Ferrara. The text of these (twenty-three in all) and of eleven letters received by the saint (five of these from the Princess of Savoy and five from John Casimir of Poland) are published by Montanari (pp. 81–90, XXIII–XLIII).

Some sayings and proverbs of the saint are collected by Bernino (chapter XXX) and Montanari (pp. IX–XXII).

Montanari has also edited the poems and songs composed by or attributed to St. Joseph of Copertino (pp. XLIII–LXXIX).

ST. JOSEPH OF COPERTINO

CHAPTER I

THE " SUPERNAL VOCATION " (PHIL. 3, 14)

Copertino, the birthplace of our saint, is situated on the peninsula of Apulia, half-way between the Gulf of Taranto and the Strait of Otranto. In the seventeenth century the town belonged to the province of Otranto, Kingdom of Naples.

But few particulars are recorded regarding the parents of St. Joseph, Felix Desa and Frances Penara. Felix was a carpenter. Kind of heart, he had given security for the debts of others. As often happens, the debtors defaulted and the creditors seized Desa's house and would have had him imprisoned had he not fled to a holy place which enjoyed the right of asylum. Meanwhile the mother of our saint fled from her home and, unable to reach the house of a friend, took refuge in a stable.[1] Here, on June 17, 1603, a child was born. He was baptized in the church of our

[1] Gattari, 1.

Lady of the Snow [2] and received the name of Joseph Mary. [3]

As a child Joseph was a spirited lad and inclined to anger. His mother strove to repress his exuberance of spirit and all manifestations of undue boldness by stern rebuke and kind admonition. She was so severe that in after years the saint used to say he needed no novitiate as a religious because he had passed a novitiate under his mother. [4]

These efforts of the pious mother bore abundant fruit. Joseph delighted in visiting the churches of his native city. At home he erected a little altar, before which he spent part of the day and the night reciting rosaries and Litanies. At the age of eight he experienced his first ecstasies. When, at school, he would hear the organ or the songs the teacher practised with the more advanced scholars, he would let his book fall and remain immovable with eyes raised to heaven and lips parted. Owing to this his companions called him " bocca aperta," " open mouth." [5]

About this time [6] Joseph was afflicted with pain-

[2] Bernino, 3.   [3] Gattari, 2.   [4] Bernino, 3.   [5] Bernino, 4–5.
[6] " When little more than seven years " (Bernino, 5); " from 8–14 " (Daumer, 45).

ful ulcers. This trial he bore with extraordinary patience, seeking no other relief than the consolation of Holy Mass. Unable to walk, he entreated his mother to carry him in her arms to the church every morning. A hermit of some repute as a healer, who lived near the church of our Lady of Grace in Galatone, endeavored to cure the child by employing the surgical means then in vogue,[7] but to no purpose; long neglect had seemingly rendered the malady incurable. After four years of suffering God intervened. One day when the hermit had applied to the ulcers some oil taken from a lamp kept burning before an image of our Lady of Grace, the boy suddenly felt relieved from all pain. With the aid of a cane he was then able to walk from the church of our Lady of Galatone to Copertino, a distance of nine miles. Before his cure he could visit the hermit only by lying helpless on a horse led by his mother. It need hardly be said that the boy showed his gratitude by an increased love of God and greater zeal in His service.

In his youth our saint was apprenticed to a cob-

[7] "Col ferro, e col fuoco"; this would suggest cauterizing; according to Daumer (46) the diseased flesh was removed by forfices.

bler.[8] Cardinal Brancati has recorded many of
the pious practices of this period of Joseph's life.
Such were his frequent visits to various churches,
assistance at Holy Mass and the wearing of a painful cilice. He abstained from all fleshmeat, and
contented himself with vegetables, which he sea-
soned with wormwood to give them a bitter taste.
His fasts were so severe that he would at times
abstain from all food for two or three consecutive
days. His body was thus weakened, but his spirit
was so lifted up to God that, when asked why he
had eaten nothing, he would reply with charming
grace, " I did not think of it."

With the years there grew upon Joseph a desire
to leave the deceitful world and unite himself
more closely to God. Feeling a great attraction
to the Order of Conventuals, he applied for assistance to his paternal uncle, Father Francis Desa,
a religious of that Order. This priest, however,
regarded his nephew as unfit for the exalted dignity of the priesthood because of his lack of edu-
cation, and was unwilling to assist him. In spite
of this refusal Joseph persevered in his resolve to
enlist under the banner of the holy patriarch St.

[8] Bernino, 8.

Francis, whom to follow he felt called by a continued inspiration of God. He therefore humbly requested Father Antony of Francavilla,[9] Provincial of the Capuchins, to receive him into the Order as a lay-brother. His request was granted and he received the habit, taking the name of Stephen, in the monastery at Martina in August,[10] 1620.

The path of the novice was beset with difficulties. He was employed in the kitchen and refectory, but displayed a woeful lack of ability. At times he could not distinguish wheat bread from rye bread, often he broke dishes by letting them fall, upset pots in putting wood on the fire and committed other blunders of a similar nature. Some have ascribed this awkwardness to a defect of sight. Another and truer explanation is that his surroundings inflamed him with the fire of divine love to such a degree that his soul was continually enraptured. God, whose ways are wonderful, permitted that after a trial of eight months Joseph was dismissed from the novitiate and deprived of the habit. This pained him so much that in after years he said, " It seemed to me as if

[9] Bernino, 13. [10] Bernino, ibid.

my skin was torn off with the habit and my flesh rent from the bones."

Little care had been taken of Joseph's secular apparel since his investment. His hat and shoes and stockings were not forthcoming, and bare of head and foot he set out for Vetrara, where his uncle, Father Francis Desa,[11] was then preaching the Lenten sermons. By thus avoiding Copertino he meant to escape ridicule and reproach.

On the way he encountered great dangers. A number of savage shepherd-dogs set upon him. The shepherds came to his aid but, owing to his unusual guise, suspected him of being a spy of the banditti and were about to lay violent hands on him when, fortunately, one of them recognized him. They then spoke kindly to him and gave him some bread. Finally a horseman of terrific form appeared to him with a sword in his hand, crying, " Halt, spy! " as if he were a spy of the royal government. Hardly had the saint gone a few steps farther when, on turning about, he found the rider had disappeared from the vast plain, and said to himself, " It was Malatasca [12] [a name also used by St. Catharine of

[11] Gattari, 5.
[12] This word was also used by Bl. Veronica of Binasco

Siena to denote the evil one], who wished to frighten me and drive me to despair."

On his arrival at Vetrara he prostrated himself before his uncle and patiently bore his reproaches of "good-for-nothing" and "vagabond." To his uncle's query as to his strange attire and visit, he replied in simple humility, "The Capuchin Fathers have taken the habit from me because I am good for nothing." Moved by compassion, his uncle kept him till Easter (which in that year fell on April 11) [13] and then secretly brought him to Copertino. Joseph bore with invincible patience the upbraidings of his mother, who treated him with apparent severity, but in her heart loved him dearly. With tears she besought the civil authorities not to imprison him because of the debts of his father, who had died. Assisted by Father Francis Desa, Father John Donatus,[14] and other friars of the convent at Grottella, she finally obtained his admission as tertiary into the Order of Conventuals.[15]

and St. Mary Magdalen de' Pazzi. "Malatasca" literally means evil sack (Acta Sanctorum, Sept. V, 1017).

[13] Acta Sanct., 1, c., 994.

[14] Gattari, 6.

[15] The date of this investment is uncertain (Acta Sanct., p. 1010).

To Joseph the investment as tertiary was a source of happiness, even though he was employed in tending the mule and in other servile occupations about the monastery. After some time he was appointed associate of his maternal uncle, Father John Donatus, a religious of great piety and learning. His new duties served to augment in his heart the flame of divine love. When he was sent out to gather alms for the needs of the monastery, the people were moved by his poor habit, his modest conduct, the charm and simplicity of his kind words, and so gave freely and generously. At the same time he aroused in them a horror of sin, zeal for virtue, and love of God. Within the monastery, his life was one of humble perseverance in lowly and fatiguing labor and of ready obedience at the word, or even beck, of each religious. To mortify his body he wore not only a cilice, but, in addition, an iron chain about his loins. He fasted strictly without intermission and, to gain more time for prayer, slept but little and this on a bed which consisted of three boards, a much-worn bearskin and a rough pallet of straw.

God's design was that Joseph should become a priest in the Order of Conventuals. The religious regarded the pious tertiary with favor, and at the Provincial Chapter held at Altamura, he was received into the Order as a cleric, June 19, 1625. He retained his baptismal name, Joseph, and joyfully began his novitiate in the monastery at Grottella.

With great earnestness he endeavored to live for God alone and to acquire the knowledge necessary for the priesthood. He attained to a high degree of perfection by his withdrawal from all association with men in order to commune uninterruptedly with God in meditation. Other means which he employed, were humility, patience, and obedience. Regarding himself as the most despicable sinner on earth, he often said he had received the habit out of pure mercy. He patiently bore the severest reproaches for faults he had never committed. With alacrity he executed the most difficult and seemingly impossible tasks, which his superiors imposed on him to probe his virtue. To this obedience was added severe mortification of the flesh, in short, the practice of all virtues, which in time led his fellow religious to consider him as a model of holiness.

In studies Joseph made but little progress and

was therefore often harshly rebuked by his novice-master, to whom he would reply, " Have patience with me, you will thus acquire merit."   In spite of his poor progress in learning he was admitted to solemn vows because of his great virtue and made his profession amid tears of joy.

Trusting in God and his holy Mother, whose powerful aid he had frequently implored, he received minor orders without previous exam-ination, January 30, 1627, subdeaconship Feb-ruary 27, of the same year, and deaconship March 20.   The examination on the latter occa-sion he passed in a providential manner; for the passage of the Gospel beginning with the words, " Blessed is the womb that bore thee," which the Bishop of Nardo gave him to explain, was the only one he had learned by long study and could well interpret.[16]   He was finally ordained priest March 28, 1628, by the Rt. Rev. John Baptist Detti, Bishop of Castro.   This prelate was so pleased with the learning of the friars whom he had examined first, that he considered the others, among whom was Joseph, to be equally well pre-pared, and ordained them without examination.

[16] Because of this occurrence St. Joseph is invoked as patron of examinations by students in Italy and France (Gattari, 171–172).

CHAPTER II

"AS GOLD IN A FURNACE" (WISD. 3, 6)

After ordination Joseph returned to the monastery at Grottella and before the image, which is venerated there, humbly thanked our Blessed Lady for the dignity of the priesthood. He said his first Holy Mass with great fervor and lively faith, and was favored with heavenly enlightenment. On touching the sacred body of Jesus Christ he was seized with a holy dread and, believing himself unworthy of so sublime an office, he prayed for purity of heart and hands. Prompted by great love of God, he resolved anew to die entirely to the world and to lead a supernatural life.

To have left the companionship of men for a narrow and dark cell seemed to the saint a small sacrifice, and so he likewise left the company of his brothers in religion. He often retired to a small room above the vault of the church, or to a chapel dedicated to St. Barbara in an olive-grove near the monastery, and there prayed unceasingly, meditated on divine things, and experienced sweet ecstasies and rapturous flights. Not only during the sixteen years of his stay at Grottella, but during his whole life, these ecstasies and flights were so frequent, as attested in the acts of the process of beatification, that for more than thirty-five years his superiors would not permit him to take part in the exercises in the choir and the refectory or in processions, lest he disturb the community.

To avoid interruptions in the narrative, and for the sake of brevity, a later chapter will treat of these ecstasies.   Now we shall describe his virtuous life at Grottella.

With heroic fortitude Joseph deprived himself of the few utensils and objects which religious are allowed for personal use, by giving them to his superior.   All superfluous garments he likewise disposed of and, casting himself at the foot of a crucifix, he prayed: "Look upon me, Lord; I am divested of all things, Thou art my only good, I regard all else as a danger and ruin to my soul."

About this time he felt such sadness of heart and such privation of heavenly consolation that he suffered agonies, and this trial continued two full years. Finally God deigned to comfort His servant, who had remained faithful to him in so great a trial. One day, when, feeling far removed from all help and, lying on his bed, he cried out, amid many sobs and tears: "My Lord, why hast Thou forsaken me?" a stranger in religious garb, whom he believed to be an angel, suddenly stood before him and gave him a new habit. Hardly had Joseph put on this habit, when all sadness passed away and joyousness of heart returned.

The saint severely chastised his body in order to subject it to the spirit. During his priestly life he abstained from bread for five years, from wine for ten years, and ate only herbs, dried fruits and beans, to which he added a powder, which several religious who tasted it described as of unspeakable bitterness. The vegetables which he ate on Fridays were of such repugnant savor that a friar who tasted them with the tip of his tongue, was so sickened that for several days all food caused him nausea.

The saint's fast was practically uninterrupted; for he observed the seven fasts of forty days each, practised by St. Francis, so strictly that for the most part he abstained from all food except on

Sundays and Thursdays. He sustained life by the " Bread of Angels," which was his daily food. No matter how faint he felt before receiving Holy Communion, after receiving he was strong and of healthy color. His weakened stomach could bear no meat, and once, when he ate some out of obedience, he had to vomit. At times his throat would close, so that he could take food only with difficulty.

He slept little, and this on a bed which was more a bed of pain than a place of rest. He continually lacerated his body with a scourge studded with needles, pins, and star-shaped pieces of steel, which caused him to lose so much blood that the walls of his cell and the other places, already mentioned, to which he withdrew, were seen to be sprinkled and, as it were, covered with blood. In addition to these scourgings he used a cilice and chain and a large flat piece of iron, which so tightened the cilice and chain that they penetrated into the flesh. One day his superior found him covered with wounds, and noticing that he could hardly breathe, commanded him to relinquish these instruments of penance. By this manner of life Joseph became a prodigy of all virtues and was made worthy to enjoy an excess of divine favors, ecstasies and flights, frequent miracles and other heavenly gifts.

The fame of our saint spread abroad, especially after he had been appointed associate of the Father Provincial on all his journeys in the province of Bari. On such occasions the people came from far and near to see him, to hear his teachings and implore his prayers. He was usually called the apostle of the country, and all places he visited experienced the effects of his great charity.

A Vicar-General, not knowing the saintliness of Joseph, accused him before the Inquisition at Naples. The accusation was that he went about attracting the people to himself as to another Messias, and at every turn performed works which the credulous believed to be miracles.

The Inquisition accordingly directed the Father Guardian at Grottella to send Father Joseph to Naples. Three years before a religious had asked Joseph whether he would like to go to Naples, and in reply the saint had predicted that in course of time he would go thither, but at the command of the Holy Office. Shortly before his summons to Naples, Jesus forewarned him of his impending trial by appearing to him during meditation in the form of a child, poorly clad, and carrying a large cross on his shoulder. At another time, when Joseph had erected several crosses on the way from Grottella to Copertino to stimulate devotion, he heard a voice saying: "Leave alone the dead crosses and take hold of the living ones."

On receiving the letter of the Holy Office, Joseph humbly set out for Naples, October 21, 1638.[1] The inhabitants of Copertino deplored his departure and said: "Alas, what a loss for us." Joseph, however, left with a peaceful heart and joyful countenance and, amid ecstasies and sufferings, arrived at Naples and took up his abode in the monastery of Saint Lawrence. Here he found the religious, who well knew the cause of his journey, in great consternation. They received him unwillingly, and the saint was much distressed that he, though innocent, should cause anxiety to his fellow-religious.

Sad of heart he went next morning with his usual companion, Brother Louis, to the building of the Inquisition, but on the way he was joined by a young religious of graceful and comely appearance, who encouraged and comforted him.

[1] Bernino, 87.

When Joseph was about to enter the palace of
the Inquisition he no longer saw the youth, and
as Brother Louis affirmed that he had not seen
him, Joseph believed that St. Antony had appeared to strengthen him.   It was therefore with
a cheerful spirit that he presented himself before
the sacred tribunal.   He was detained several
weeks and examined three times, but no shadow
of fault was discovered and his life was found
to be worthy of admiration.   On seeing him
dismissed so soon and with such honor, his
brethren in religion rejoiced much that his holiness had stood the test and had been found pure
and free from hypocrisy.

After this his piety became better known, so
that many people of Naples, even nobles, came to
see him and make his acquaintance.   Joseph alone
did not share this high opinion of his person, but
styled himself a " sinner, who knew not how to
live with his brethren in religion and deserved to
remain with the beasts of burden."   This he said
to the nuns of St. Ligorio at Naples.   At the command of the Inquisition he had said Mass in their
church, dedicated to St. Gregory of Armenia, and
there was raised in ecstasy above the altar.   This
occurrence so increased the fame of his holiness

that it penetrated to the royal palace, and the Viceroy with his wife and court wished him to say Mass in their chapel. Difficulties intervened, the function was postponed, and in the meantime the saint left the city and thus evaded the contemplated honor.

CHAPTER III

Upon the command of the Holy Office Joseph
had left Naples for Rome with important mes-
sages for the Father General of the Order. During this journey his spirit was absorbed in contemplation of divine things. On seeing the holy
city, the center of the Catholic world, he desired
to enter it in poverty after the example of his holy
Father, St. Francis. When, therefore, they had
come to the walls of the city, he bade his companion, Brother Louis, to lay their last piece of
money, a small silver coin, on a stone for the
benefit of the first one who should pass.

When Joseph arrived at the monastery of the
Twelve Apostles within the city, the Father General, John Baptist Berardicelli,[1] who had never
before met him, received him at first with great
reserve and forbidding mien; for the message of

[1] Gattari, 29.

the Holy Office directed him to send Joseph to some solitary monastery. The General had the most secluded room of the monastery assigned to him with the injunction to remain there till further disposition were made. The General had in mind to send him to one of the smallest and most secluded monasteries. Meanwhile it pleased God to reward the humble resignation of His servant amid such great and painful trials by revealing his holiness not only to his brethren in religion, but even to the Cardinals and the Supreme Head of the Church, Pope Urban VIII.[2] The Pope commanded the Father General to send Father Joseph to a monastery in which the rule was most perfectly observed. This caused the Father General to alter his plans and to send Joseph to the monastery at Assisi. The command gave the saint great pleasure, for he had long desired to live near the tomb of his holy Father, St. Francis. Without delay he therefore set out with Brother Louis and full of joy arrived at Assisi the last day of April, 1639.[3]

Joseph's joy was of short duration; for God wished to try His servant anew, and, as it were, by fire, by withdrawal of consolation, by persecu-

[2] Gattari, 30. [3] Gattari, 32.

BASILICA OF ST. FRANCIS AT ASSISI. TOMB OF ST. FRANCIS

tions, temptations and spiritual dryness which should purify his soul more effectively than the earlier trials at Grottella. Soon after Joseph's arrival at Assisi Father Antony of St. Maure was appointed Custos of the place. Although, as Provincial of the Province of Bari, he had tenderly loved Joseph and taken him for his companion, he now (certainly not without the design of heaven) changed his conduct. He treated the pious Joseph at first with haughtiness, then with contempt, and finally threatened and repeatedly punished him, calling him a useless hypocrite and publicly reproving him as such. The courageous saint regarded all this as a source of merit, and not only bore these bitter reproaches and accusations in silence, but evinced even greater humility and greater readiness to serve his superior.

In addition to these trials on the part of the Custos, the Lord began gradually to withdraw the consolations which had heretofore given Joseph courage. The saint had no longer either ecstasies or heavenly delights; on the contrary, he experienced aridity during spiritual reading, when praying the Divine Office, at the Holy Sacrifice of the Mass, in short, in all divine things. God seemed to be deaf to his voice, unmoved by his tears, insensible to his requests, so that poor Joseph was oppressed by a deep gloom, which seemed to break his heart and manifested itself in his dim and tired eyes.

The devil frequently assailed the saint with terrible temptations, suggesting to him impure thoughts and disturbing his sleep by most hideous dreams.   To these assaults, which lasted almost two years, Joseph, though terrified, offered continual resistance, so that the inner citadel of his soul remained firm and unshaken, God's superabundant grace strengthening him in keeping with the severity of his sufferings.

Remembering the delights of spirit he had enjoyed when near our Lady of Grottella, whom he was wont to call his mother, Joseph thought of returning thither.   To a fellow-religious he said, " I should like to return to our Lady of Grottella, for she is my mother."   The Father General, however, learning of Joseph's unrest, summoned him to Rome to keep him there during the whole of Lent, 1644.[4]

While on the way with his companion, he was seized with a great desire to return to his beloved shrine of the Blessed Virgin and thought of ask-

[4] Bernino, 127.

ing his superior for leave to go. In his soul, however, he heard the voice of God chiding him because of this innocent but vain desire, and saying: "What desirest thou? What seekest thou? What demandest thou? Am I not the same here as there?" Enlightened by these words, Joseph stood still, raised his eyes to heaven and said to his companion, "My brother, we shall soon return to Assisi." And, indeed, after a brief stay at Rome, where God again opened to him His bountiful hand and made him partake of heavenly sweetness in ecstasies of love, Joseph returned to Assisi.

His return was a source of joy to the religious and the citizens of Assisi. On his arrival he was led into the church and, seeing on the ceiling a picture of Our Lady similar to that at Grottella, he cried, "Ah, my dear Mother, you have followed me," and was lifted about eighteen paces into the air, as if to embrace the picture. Several days later, on seeing a true copy of the Virgin of Grottella, which Father Michaelangelo Catalano, Assistant to the General, gave to him, he repeated the ejaculation, "Ah, my Mother!" hastened toward the picture, and with his eyes fixed upon it remained a long time in delightful ecstasy.

Joseph was now formally adopted into the family of the Conventuals of the Sacro Convento.[5]   The city council by unanimous vote conferred on him honorary citizenship, and a delegation was sent to present to him the diploma.[6] The saint received the delegates in his cell and so delighted was he to become a " fellow-citizen of St. Francis," as he expressed himself, that he was robbed of the use of his senses and lifted in ecstasy almost to the ceiling.

[5] "Honore di gran distinzione " (Bernino, 134).

[6] The wording of the diploma, dated Aug. 4, 1644, is given by Montanari, pp. 190–192.

CHAPTER IV

Calm had now followed the storm, and a love so powerful and tender possessed our saint, that his noble soul seemed united more to God than to the body and, as it were, immersed in a limitless ocean of love. Owing to this love it happened that, whenever he heard songs or music in church, or a conversation about God, or the names of Jesus and Mary, he would be enraptured and cry out, " O love, O love!" or would sing sacred songs. Among these was one to St. Catharine of Siena, whom he venerated as his special patron. When, in the song, he came to the words, " and the divine love pierced her hands and feet, and even her heart," [1] he would weep, tremble all over, and, with a corresponding gesture, say, " Open my breast, cleave this heart." To the question, what he desired most, he replied, " That God take my heart, my whole heart." Before an

[1] This song was composed by the saint; the full text is given by Montanari, LII-LIII.

image of the Crucified Saviour he would often pray, " I desire to be dissolved and to be with Christ," or " Jesus, Jesus, Jesus, draw me to Thee, I cannot remain here; sweetest Jesus, draw me up to where Thou art."

In the holy season of Christmas, the saint joyfully invited all to sing with him the song: " Bambino, my Bambino, give, oh, give to me but a small share of Thy divine love." [2]   At times, especially during Holy Week, he was sad and, on meeting anyone, would lament and say, " Think of it, my son, Jesus has been scourged, Jesus has been crucified, Jesus has died and has died for love." After various other ejaculations, he would usually conclude with the words, " I am much worse than the Jews; for I know who Thou art, and yet crucify Thee." On such days he pined away in sorrow and lay as dead in a swoon. But when Easter came, he sang and exulted for hours together for joy, and on Pentecost he would glow with the same divine fire and display a like jubilation of spirit.

By such manifestations of holy love he aroused similar sentiments in the hearts of others and

[2] This is another song of the saint; see Montanari, LVIII.

endeavored to stimulate them still more by saying to them, "Love God; for he who loves is rich without knowing it." His desire was that the whole world should love God. He therefore wept on seeing how men offend God by so many sins and because of this felt such agony that blood gushed from his mouth. Gladly would he have shed his blood in martyrdom and, to accomplish this, desired to accompany some missionary as companion and servant to the heathen. Wishing to see all have a like desire, he would ask each religious, even the novices, "Would you gladly die for Jesus Christ?" and, when they answered in the affirmative, he would exult in his heart and manifest unusual joy.

The saint's love at times found expression in words that show his desire to be utterly unselfish.[3] "My Lord," said he, "even if I knew that

---

[3] In judging of these expressions it is well to remember that the Church has repeatedly (Innocent XI, 1687, Innocent XII, 1699) condemned the pretence of an habitual love of God in this life which excludes the fear of hell and the desire for heaven. Even the saints have made only single acts of such love, which are useful as a weapon in certain temptations. On this difficult subject see Jos. Deharbe, S. J., Die vollkommene Liebe Gottes . . . nach der Lehre des hl. Thomas von Aquin, Ratisbon, 1856, pp. 44–67, 179–200. In such acts of perfect love heaven, as

Thou hadst predestined me to hell at my creation, yet I would follow Thee in every possible way and serve Thee by all such works as have been practised by the greatest saints of paradise." In this event he would have wished to be alone, so as not to hear the blasphemies and curses of others. He therefore added, " I would wish to be in a place apart, so that I should not hear the others blaspheme and curse; in that solitary place I would bless and praise God in spite of hell."

This love, of which Pseudo-Dionysius says that it is the cause of ecstasies, was the inexhaustible

a motive of imperfect love, is disregarded (p. 200). "Hell," in such sayings, "does not imply the loss of grace and God's friendship or the punishment of despair and separation from God" (p. 184). This and other suppositions, which are impossible of realization because God will not alter the present economy of salvation, enter into these acts. These acts express a transcendent desire to please God and give us a glimpse of the purity and sublimity of love to which saints attain (66–67, 185). Bossuet erred by denying to single acts such perfection of unselfishness (192, note 2). The desire for heaven in holy souls arises mostly from perfect love, and thus becomes an act of perfect love (197). "St. Joseph of Copertino avowed that he served God neither from a desire of paradise nor from fear of hell, but because He is worthy of love and service; nevertheless his heart burned with an eager desire for heaven, and he often sang a song he had composed to express this longing" (190).

fountain from which the heart of Joseph drank
and was filled and, as it were, intoxicated with
ecstatic delight.

Divine love had influenced the soul of Joseph
from earliest childhood, and as a boy he experienced the first impulses of rapture, which later,
when he had become a priest, grew to deepest ecstasies. These recurred until his death and often
followed one another at such brief intervals that
one might regard them as continual. The least
thing pertaining to God sufficed to cause him to
cry out and to lose the use of his senses. No
doubt could be entertained as to the truth and
vehemence of this influence of divine love; for,
when pricked with needles, struck with iron, burnt
with a torch, or touched on the apple of the eye
with the tips of the fingers, he did not move in
the least and only returned to the use of his senses
when God allowed him a respite or obedience
called him. These ecstasies were so astonishing
and frequent that hardly any other saint is known
to have received of God such a superabundance in
this regard.

To satisfy the curiosity of the reader and to
make this narrative at once brief and clear, we
shall now relate some of the many ecstatic flights

in the order of time as they occurred in the various places where he lived. We begin with Copertino.

Once, on Christmas eve, when Joseph heard the sound of the bagpipes and flutes of some shepherds, whom he had invited to celebrate with him the birth of the Heavenly Child, he began to dance because of excessive joy and, with a sob and a loud cry, flew as a bird through the air from the middle of the church to the high altar, a distance of almost forty feet.[4] There he remained about a quarter of an hour in sweet rapture, without, however, disturbing any of the many lighted candles or burning his clothes. The shepherds marvelled exceedingly.

Great was the wonderment of the religious and the people of Copertino on the occasion of a procession on the feast of St. Francis. Joseph, dressed in a surplice, rose up to the pulpit, about fifteen palms from the floor, and remained a long time suspended in ecstasy with outstretched arms and bent knees. Marvellous, too, was his rapture during the night of Holy Thursday while

[4] "Più di cinque canne." The measure "canna" varied in different localities. (Acta Sanct., p. 1041.) A fair equivalent would perhaps be 7½ ft.

praying with other religious before the holy sepulchre, which was erected above the high altar and
lit with many lamps.   Suddenly he rose in direct
flight to the chalice, in which his Divine Treasure
was enclosed, but without touching any of the
many decorations, and only after some time, when
called by his superior, did he return to his former
place.

At times he made similar flights to the altar of
St. Francis or, while praying the Litany, to that
of our Lady of Grottella.   Very remarkable was
his exuberance of love when the saint erected a
Calvary on a hill between Copertino and the monastery at Grottella.   Two crosses were already
placed, but ten persons with united effort could
not raise the third, which was fifty-four palms
high and very heavy.   On seeing this Joseph,
full of ardor, flew about eighty paces from the
portal of the monastery to the cross, lifted it as
easily as if it were a straw, and placed it in the
hole prepared for it.   These crosses were the object of his special devotion, and from a distance
of ten or twelve paces, he, drawn by his crucified
Saviour, would rise to one of the arms or the top
of the cross.   One day a religious was speaking
with the saint about the descent of the Holy

Ghost on the Apostles. Just then a friar happened to pass with a burning candle in his hand, at sight of which Joseph uttered a cry and flew four paces into the air, inflamed with the fire of the Holy Ghost.[5]   Another time, hearing a priest say, " Father Joseph, oh, how beautiful God has made heaven," he flew up on an olive-tree and remained there half an hour kneeling, and it was a strange sight to see how the branch which bore him swayed as lightly as if a small bird rested on it.

On one occasion Joseph was present at the investment of several nuns in the church of St. Clare at Copertino.   As soon as the choir intoned the antiphon, " Come, thou bride of Christ," he was seen to hurry from the corner in which he knelt towards the confessor of the convent, a member of the Order of the Reformati, grasp him by the hand, lift him by supernatural power from the floor, and rapidly dance about with him in the air.   It would lead too far to recount all the raptures and flights through the air while the saint was at Copertino ; suffice it to say that, according to the acts of his beatification, more than seventy such flights were recorded, not counting

[5] See Bernino, 330.

those which occurred daily at Holy Mass and generally lasted two hours.

After the saint left Copertino, the same fire
of love burned within him and manifested itself
in the same miraculous manner.   It may interest
the pious reader to learn of some of the many
other raptures which, till the end of his life, were
an object of the greatest admiration wherever he
lived.   At Nardo, where he stayed for a time
after leaving Copertino, he was seen to be lifted
up in ecstasy in the church of St. Francis to the
terror of those present.   Another time, on seeing
an " Ecce Homo " picture, he remained immovable as a statue in a house whither he had gone to
heal a sick person.   In another house, on hearing
a song, he rose with his customary cry to a kneeling posture on the edge of a table.   Later, when
he came to Monopoli on his way to Naples, and
was led by his fellow-religious to the monastery
church to see a new and beautiful statue of St.
Antony of Padua, he rose at sight of it from the
floor and flew a distance of fifteen paces to the
image of the saint on the altar and returned in
like manner to his former place.   But scarcely
had he recovered from his first rapture when he
fell into a second; for, while the Litany was being

recited, he flew to the altar of the Immaculate
Conception and back through the air to his original place.

The city of Naples likewise witnessed his wonderful flights.   One day when, at the command
of the Inquisition, he had said Mass in the private
chapel of the church of St. Gregory of Armenia,
belonging to the nuns of St. Ligorio, he suddenly
rose with a loud cry from a corner of the chapel,
where he was praying, flew up to the altar, and
remained standing there, bending over the flowers
and candles with arms spread in the form of a
cross, so that the nuns cried out, " He will catch
fire!"   But, crying out anew, he returned un-
harmed to the middle of the church, whirled about
in a circle with the speed of an arrow and sang,
" O most Blessed Virgin!   O most Blessed Virgin!"

It pleased God to glorify the saint in the presence of men of the highest rank.   During his first
stay in Rome he went with the Father General to
pay homage to the Pope, Urban VIII.   While
kissing the feet of the Pontiff the saint, filled with
reverence for Jesus Christ in the person of His
Vicegerent, was enraptured and raised aloft till
the Father General's command brought him back

INTERIOR OF THE UPPER CHURCH, BASILICA
OF ST. FRANCIS AT ASSISI

to his senses.   The Pope marvelled much and said
to the Father General that if Father Joseph were
to die during his pontificate, he himself would
bear witness to this occurrence.

How often, by God's special grace, such happenings recurred during the thirteen years of his
stay at Assisi it is difficult to say.   In 1645, the
Spanish Ambassador to the Papal Court, the High
Admiral of Castile, passed through Assisi on purpose to see Joseph.   He visited the saint in his
cell.   After speaking with him he returned to the
church and said to his wife, " I have seen and
spoken with another Saint Francis."   On hearing this, his wife desired to meet Joseph, and, at
her request,[6] the Father Custos commanded him
to go up into the church and speak with the lady.
With the words, " I will obey, but know not
whether I shall be able to speak," the saint hastened to comply.   Scarcely had he entered the
church when, looking up to a statue of the Immaculate Conception on the altar, he flew about
twelve paces over the heads of those present to
the foot of the statue.   After remaining there
some time in prayer, he flew back with his customary cry and returned to his cell.   The occur-

[6] Gattari, 45.

rence amazed the Admiral, his wife, and their numerous retinue.

On another occasion Joseph terrified several painters, who remarked in his presence that they meant to paint a picture of the Immaculate Conception in his little chapel. They first heard him cry out in great agitation, " What? The Conception of the Virgin Mary? The Immaculate Conception?" and then they saw him remain for more than half an hour deprived of the use of his senses and immovable with outspread arms and eyes lifted to heaven, enraptured in contemplation of the sublime mystery.

Great was the astonishment of a priest who, in company with Joseph, once entered a village church. The priest enquired, " Do you think the Blessed Sacrament is preserved here?" As no lamp was burning, the saint replied, " Who knows?" But immediately he cried out aloud and flew towards the tabernacle, embraced it and adored the Blessed Sacrament, which he miraculously knew to be present. Several religious, whom he assisted to clean a reliquary and to fold a habit worn by St. Francis, saw him hover in the air above their heads. Others saw him suspended on a cornice in the chapel of St. Francis, sixteen

palms from the floor. One day, while a priest
was preaching to the faithful in the chapel of St.
Ursula, Joseph flew from a jalousied balcony,
which jutted out in front of the altar at some distance from the floor. He remained suspended in
a kneeling posture and, with face all radiant as
that of a seraph, fixed his eyes on the tabernacle
till, at the command of his superior, he flew back
to the balcony.[7] Great was the surprise and terror of the Father Custos on one occasion, when
solemn Vespers had been sung in honor of the
Immaculate Conception in the chapel of the novitiate. Joseph entreated the father to repeat with
him the words, " Beautiful Mary." He then
seized the father and, pressing him close and ex-
claiming with louder voice, " Beautiful Mary,
Beautiful Mary! " rose with him into the air.

To avoid prolixity, we will omit other ecstasies
and, in conclusion, relate one of the most marvellous, which was occasioned by a deranged
nobleman, Baltasar Rossi of Assisi.[8] Bound to
a chair, this nobleman was brought to Joseph, that
he might pray for his recovery. The man of God
commanded that the patient be freed and forced
to kneel in his oratory. He then touched his head

[7] Gattari, 44.   [8] Gattari, 43.

and said, " Chevalier Baltasar, doubt not, but
commend yourself to God and His holy Mother."
With these words and uttering his usual cry,
" Oh," he seized the nobleman by the hair and
lifted him from the floor as he rose in ecstasy into
the air.   The saint held him thus for a time to
the amazement of those present, who with the
nobleman, now fully restored, praised and thanked
God for working such great miracles by His servant.

CHAPTER V

These ecstasies and flights were, no doubt, effects of the divine love which burned in the heart of our saint and evidenced the union of his soul with God. Father Jerome Rodriguez, a pious and learned priest of the Society of Jesus, once said after conversing with Joseph: "He is perfectly united to God and his heart is more disposed to this union than powder is to be ignited by the smallest spark." This union was fostered by and found expression in continued prayer; almost without effort the saint raised his spirit to God, whom he found ready to enlighten and inflame him and to draw him towards Himself. It was as if in looking towards heaven he saw the beauty of paradise spread out before his eyes, as he once said to Cardinal Brancati (speaking as of a third person): "It appeared to him as if he were in the midst of a large gallery filled with beautiful and rare objects, and saw in a bright mirror hanging there, at a single glance, the forms of all things and could with certainty pronounce the hidden mysteries which it pleased God to reveal to him while this sublime union lasted." His customary cry was an effect of the inner fire which could not be confined to his breast, but forcibly broke forth from his lips, as he himself said, — though again as of a third person,—" like to powder proceeding from the cannon's mouth, causing a loud report." This great vehemence often raised with the soul the body and any object he happened to have hold of. He even sang and danced during these joyful ecstasies.

By reason of his abstraction from earthly things the saint often did not understand what others said to him, or gave answers which plainly showed that he used natural things only as a ladder to mount to the contemplation of the supernatural. Once, on a journey, he met several women, and when a religious asked him whether he recognized them, he replied, they were perhaps the Blessed Virgin, St. Clare, and St. Catharine. Other times, when asked regarding other persons, he mentioned various saints.

He was very attentive when reciting the canonical hours or saying his prayers, as is evinced by his many tears and the impression of his knees at the foot of the altar and on the floor of his oratory. He prayed with lively faith and firm hope in God and said to others, " Children, trust in God alone; for God alone can provide for you; men fail, God never fails." And again, " He who has faith, is lord of the earth." As to himself, he said that he trusted in God, and that he was like a man cast by accident on an ocean reef, where, surrounded by water, he could expect no help, but from God alone. If necessary he would remove mountains in the strength of this faith, from one end of the earth to the other.

This lively faith it was that rendered his prayers effective. He once prayed that Copertino and its territory be spared in a severe storm, and the hurricane ceased at once. At another time he prayed while a heavy downpour of rain frightened the inhabitants and threatened the vicinity of the convent at Grottella. When, after his prayer, he ran out of the church and cried, " Dragon, dragon," the clouds fled before him and the sky cleared. Once, when the heat of the sun had parched the fields near the same place, a procession was held to implore aid, and, as the saint had foretold, a plentiful rain fell immediately after. It was owing to Joseph's prayers that Alcide Fabiani, a surgeon, passed unnoticed six assassins who sought to waylay him on his return from Spello to Assisi. By his prayer he saved the Father General of his Order from the danger of drowning in a deep trench, called Cannara, near the village of Monte Falco. The father, with his frightened mule, had fallen from a bridge, and in falling had commended himself to Joseph, who was then still living. On seeing the Father General later, the saint said to him: " Certainly, my dear Father General, you were in great peril; for you had a dangerous fall at ten o'clock, just as I was saying Mass, and I prayed to God for you."

The efficacy of his prayers is strikingly shown in the conversion to the Catholic faith of a Lutheran prince, John Frederick, Duke of Brunswick. While visiting the principal courts of Europe, in the year 1649, the prince, then twenty-five years of age, came from Rome to Assisi expressly to see Joseph, of whose fame he had heard in Germany. On his arrival at the monastery, he was given lodging in the rooms reserved for persons of rank and, as he wished to speak with Joseph and then continue his journey, he, with two of his retainers (one a Catholic, the other a Protestant) was led next morning to the door of the chapel, where the servant of God was saying Mass. The saint, who was not informed of their presence, was made aware of it when about to break the sacred host, which he found so hard, that, in spite of all his efforts, he could not break it, but had to replace it on the paten. Fixing his eyes upon the host, he wept and with a loud cry rose in kneeling posture about five paces into the air. With another cry he returned after some time to the altar and broke the sacred host, though with great effort. At the instance of the Duke, the Father Superior asked him why he had wept, and he replied: "My dear compatriot,[1] the persons, whom you sent to my Mass this morning, have a hard heart; for they do not believe all that Holy Mother Church teaches, and therefore the Lamb of God was hardened in my hands so that I could not break the sacred host." The Duke, astonished at this occurrence, deferred his departure in order to consult with the servant of God. This he did after dinner, remaining with the saint till Compline. Moved by divine grace, the Duke wished again to assist at Holy Mass on the fol-

[1] "Paesano."

lowing day. At the elevation, the cross on the host appeared black to all present, and the saint, with his usual cry, was raised up a palm from the floor, and remained about a quarter of an hour in this position, elevating the host. On seeing this miracle the Duke wept, but his companion, the Lutheran, said angrily: " Cursed be the hour in which I came to this country; for at home I was much more at peace and now my conscience is tormented by the furies of doubt." [2] Joseph, enlightened from above, assured one of his friends of the future conversion of the prince in the following words, " Let us be of good cheer, the deer is wounded." The prince conversed with Joseph till midday. On seeing the Duke return to his cell after Vespers, the saint hurried towards him, girded him with his girdle, and said with great fervor: " For paradise I bind you; go, venerate St. Francis, assist at Compline, follow with devotion in the procession, and do all as you see the friars do." The prince humbly obeyed, promised to become a Catholic, and with his own hand inscribed himself in the register of

[2] Henry Julius Blume became a Catholic in 1653. See Dr. Andreas Raess, Die Convertiten seit der Reformation, vol. VI (Freiburg, Herder, 1868), pp. 450–452, 558–571.

the Archconfraternity of the Cord of St. Francis. Before publicly abjuring heresy, he returned home to arrange his affairs. The following year he came to Assisi and, as he had promised, knelt before the Blessed Sacrament, and in the presence of Cardinals Facchinetti and Rapaccioli, made profession of faith in the hands of Father Joseph. Ever after the Duke remained devoted to his benefactor.

Very numerous are the miracles God wrought through the intercession of His servant Joseph. We will content ourselves with adding these words from the process of beatification: " His prayer was never in vain, but always obtained what he implored for the welfare of the soul and body; even those who merely commended themselves to him, received the desired favor at the moment he prayed for them." Knowing that all good comes of prayer and wishing his neighbor all good, he frequently exhorted others by saying, " Pray, pray."

Joseph's charity was such that he prayed without ceasing for all men, for the just, that they might persevere in God's grace, and for sinners, that they might amend their life and do penance. To render his prayer effective, he would at times implore God to bear, as with the past, so, too, with the present sins of the world; at other times he would severely chastise his body to make atonement, in some measure, for the sins of others. When others recommended themselves to his prayers, he would kindly reply, " Take refuge to God, and I, on my part, will not fail to pray for you." When such as were troubled with doubts came to him he repeated to them the words, " Scruples and melancholy I tolerate not in my house." [3] After counselling and comforting them he would in such cases jestingly take a broom, sweep them from head to foot, and say, " See, I have taken all scruples from your back; do good, have a pure intention, and cast off all doubts." Whenever he saw or heard of dissension he was very desirous to put an end to it and usually succeeded in restoring peace.

His conversation was unaffected, yet so interesting that he captivated the hearts of all who heard him. It was his wish that all should be upright and gentle in their intercourse. He detested deceit, pride, and ostentation, and exhorted all, even his superiors, to compassion, gentleness,

[3] One of the favorite sayings of the saint; see Montanari, X.

and love. He frequently repeated such sayings as: "Love, oh, love; he who has love is rich and knows it not; who has not love, has nothing; he is unhappy without knowing it. Love and charity make for happiness." On seeing anyone perform an act of charity, he rejoiced and would even embrace such a person, as he once did a religious who had put an end to a dissension between certain persons by pacifying their anger. He said to him, "God bless you, my dear son. May St. Francis bless you; for you have acted as a true son of his."

This tender charity he recommended to others and practised himself, even towards those who offended him. One who had insulted him was rewarded by a miracle. Another who had wounded him with a knife because of a reproof, he won by gentleness and forbearance, at the same time advising him of his approaching end. Yet another, who was on the point of attacking him in anger, he tenderly embraced. Another fruit of his charity was his zeal. In the monastery he severely reprimanded those who transgressed the rule, and admonished his superiors to be vigilant. Sometimes he impetuously approached and reproved the transgressors, as once at Assisi, on seeing two persons engaged in vain discourse in the Basilica of St. Francis.

The saint sought to heal the secret wounds of the soul, which he knew by heavenly enlightenment.   Thus he freed Alphonso of Montefuscolo from temptations against chastity, which beset him, and, at Copertino, induced a lady of Veglie to burn a charm she was making.   A person of distinction once brought to him a young nobleman who was in a state of mortal sin.   The saint said: " Who is this Moor, whom you have brought to me?   Do you not see that he is black?"   Then he turned to the nobleman and said, " Go, my son, and wash your face."   When the man returned to him after a contrite confession, Joseph said: " Now, my son, you are beautiful; wash yourself frequently; yesterday you were ugly as a Moor." To everyone whose soul he saw disfigured by sin he said: " Oh, how ugly you are!   Go, adjust your bow!"   By this latter expression he meant their conscience.

As Joseph with Christian candor revealed their faults to those who had fallen into sin, that they might repent, so he kindly cared for those who were in danger of falling, or were tempted.   A priest of Spello, who was about to sully his soul

by committing a grievous sin, experienced the effects of Joseph's charity. Beset by a severe
temptation, and in imminent danger of consent-
ing, it was his good fortune to meet the saint,
who pressed his hand and kindly said to him:
"My son, resist this temptation with courage;
for it is God's will that you offend Him not; this
I say to you in earnest." By this singular admonition he assisted the priest to conquer.
Those who were tempted by evil spirits he
advised to receive the sacraments frequently.
"For," said he, "where God dwells, the enemy of
God cannot easily approach; and in the long run
God always conquers because by His grace He
can do more than the devil by temptations."

The charity of our hero was not restricted to
the faithful, whom he would lead to God, but
reached out to infidels. He spoke with great ten-
derness and compassion of their unhappy state
and would gladly have undertaken anything for
their conversion. It happened that once, when
praying for them and meditating on the inscruta-
ble mysteries of Divine Providence, he was enraptured for a long time. On coming to himself,
he wept bitterly and said to those about him:
"My children, pray for the just and the sinners,

pray for the heretics, Turks and infidels; in short, pray for all; for we are all redeemed by the most precious blood of Jesus Christ."

His charity extended also, as far as obedience would permit, to the bodily needs of his fellowmen. Even in the seclusion of his cell he knew by divine enlightenment of their wants and aided them by his prayer. Where he had full liberty to act, he hastened to the aid of the sick within and without the monastery, admonished them to resign themselves to the will of God, and cheered them by words of good counsel. With joyful countenance he would kindly say to such as feared death or were sad for other reasons, " Be of good cheer, God will provide for you." He was ever ready to render them the most humble services. He lifted them up, fed them, and bandaged their wounds. In short, his love for the sick was so great that his fellow-religious were accustomed to say, It were better to be sick than to be well when with Joseph, as in the former case he lived only for the sick, in the latter only for himself. His charity toward the sick was, moreover, so pleasing to God that He glorified the saint by miraculous cures.

The affection of his tender heart was manifested especially during a disastrous famine in Assisi and the adjoining provinces. He wept and prayed without ceasing to implore aid from God, and, as he was not allowed to beg for the support of the hungry outside the monastery, he anxiously went about within the precincts of the convent to comfort and cheer at least his spiritual brethren.

Gratitude prompted him, in view of his poverty, to reward his benefactors by thanking and blessing them, by praying for and promising ever to remember them. Once he spoke winningly to a surgeon who had rendered him aid: " Be blessed for the great kindness you have shown me; God will reward you for it, and I will not forget to pray for you when I shall come to the abode of the blessed."

Joseph's gratitude towards the Blessed Virgin Mary, to whose intercession he ascribed all benefits he received from God, was most extraordinary. He sought to show her a love than which none could be more tender and deep. In infancy his mother instilled into him devotion towards Mary. He was accustomed to call Mary his mother. It is difficult to tell how eagerly he served and honored her. He adorned her images

with flowers and devoted the most fervent affec-
tions of his heart to her. He was wont to say
jestingly: " My mother is very strange; if I
bring her flowers, she says she does not want
them; if I bring her cherries, she will not take
them, and if I then ask her what she desires, she
replies: 'I desire thy heart; for I live on
hearts!'" That his heart belonged to Mary was
apparent from the continued devout prayers
which he recited in her honor and the tender
words he applied to her, calling her his protectress,
lady, patroness, mother and helper, from the simple and joyful songs with which he extolled her,
and especially from the frequent ecstasies and
flights which he experienced when he saw her
image or heard her praises.

Once, when the Litany of our Lady was being
prayed in the church, he flew over six fellow-
religious at the words " Holy Mary." At other
times such flights occurred at the words, " Holy
Mother of God," " Mother of Divine Grace,"
" Gate of Heaven." Even on hearing the name
of Mary he was often enraptured and lifted from
the ground. His heart melted at the thought of
the beauty of the Queen of Heaven. One day,
while he was saying Mass, many persons saw him

enraptured and lifted into the air and heard him exclaim with tears in his eyes, " Praise her, ye holy angels, with your songs; for I pine away because I cannot worthily praise her."

Not satisfied that Mary should be loved and praised by all the saints and angels of Paradise, he most earnestly desired that she be loved and praised by all men on earth. Some citizens of Copertino once came to the monastery at Grottella to visit him. " Why have you come?" he said to them. " Do you wish to visit Our Lady?" When they replied in the affirmative, he continued, " And what have you brought?" They replied, " The Office and the rosary." " What Office? What rosary?" he asked,— for he well knew they had come out of curiosity. " My Lady wishes more, she desires the heart and the will." By these words he inflamed their hearts with love for Mary and, bidding them kneel, prayed the Litany with them as he was accustomed to do with all who came to his cell. He also admonished all to repeat often the words: " Mary, thou refuge of sinners, Mother of God, be mindful of me." This ejaculatory prayer, he said, pleased the Blessed Virgin very much because she is justly called Refuge of Sinners.

Joseph sought to honor the Mother of God by the frequent recital of the praises contained in the Litany of Loreto. Once, when the shepherds with whom he prayed the Litany each Saturday in a chapel near the monastery at Grottella, were hindered from coming, he called with a loud voice to the sheep which he could see from afar, " Come hither, to revere the mother of your God and my God." At these words the sheep, which were so far distant from Joseph that his voice could not have reached them, ran towards the chapel, without regarding the cries of the shepherd boys, and when they had come to the chapel, the saint joyfully began the Litany. The animals replied in their own way to each praise which he uttered, so that, for instance, when he said " Holy Mary," all cried " Baa " and in this manner completed the Litany. On receiving the saint's blessing, they gambolled back to their pastures.

The servant of God had acquired such confidence in his heavenly Mother that by reciting the Litany he was able to exorcise devils and free the possessed. In serious dissensions he reconciled the litigants by saying to them, " Let us go to Mother, to Mother." In the name of the

Mother of God, to whom he ascribed all good, he frequently promised to work miracles and occasionally wrought them without delay. Thus he once cured a blind woman by touching her eyes and saying: " May the Mother of God restore you to health." The Vicar-General of Nardo was unwilling to bless the three crosses which Joseph had erected near Grottella because of the great heat, but acceded to the entreaties of the saint when he said, " My Mother will not let you feel the heat." Although the solemnity lasted three and one half hours and the Vicar-General wore a cope, he did not feel the least discomfort from the broiling sun.

At times Joseph's mother, who was poor, came to seek his aid. To her he said: " The Madonna is my mother. I have nothing because I am poor. Take refuge to the Madonna, she will provide for you." In very deed she always gave opportune aid in some mysterious way. To a priest who was confined to bed by ulcers he said, " Do not lose courage; how long is it since you were at Grottella to see your Mother? " " Alas," replied the sick man, " do you not see in what condition I am and that I can hardly move? " The servant of God then bandaged his

wounds and stroked them saying, " Have you no
confidence in your Mother?" At the same moment the ulcers dried up and healed, and soon the
priest recovered fully. Another priest hesitated
to pray for a particular grace. The saint, seeing the cause of his doubt, said to him, " Take
refuge to Mary; she will hear you." The prayer
was heard. At another time the saint opened the
lips of a dying man and, as he gave him a certain
liquid to drink, asked him, " Do you feel better
now?" The man replied, " Yes," and Joseph
continued, " Then say nothing about me to anyone, but rather say the Mother of God, who is
your mother and mine, has made you well."

To be brief, Joseph's holiness began, as he himself attested, with devotion to Mary. The fame
of his holiness was likewise due to the many
graces which people received from Mary because
of his prayer. During his whole life our saint
called the Blessed Virgin " Mother," and in dying
he invoked her by that sweet name in the words
of the Ave Maris Stella:

> Show thyself a Mother;
> Offer Him our sighs,
> Who for us Incarnate
> Did not thee despise.

CHAPTER VI

EVANGELICAL PERFECTION

The love of our saint for the virtue of purity may be measured by his love for the "Mother most pure." He was not immune, as were some saints, from impure temptations, but rather severely molested by them; but the more vehement the temptations, the more glorious was the victory which he won by invoking the aid of God and the B. V. Mary. Nevertheless, he was so disquieted by doubts and fears that he was once heard to exclaim: "Alas, my God, I know that Thou hast made all things well and that by Thy grace I shall not sin in these temptations, but I would wish not to experience them." It was God's will, however, that he be not free from temptations, yet remain pure and unsullied. His confessors and many others have testified that they never remarked in him even a shadow of impurity, but rather found him wholly pure in body and soul, so that his spirit appeared to them more angelic than human.

In his love for purity, and in order to lead others to esteem it, he was wont to say that a pure soul was like a crystal vase, beautifully polished and filled with fresh, clear water, which everybody prizes in the time of heat; but if only a single drop of oil were poured in, the whole mass of water would become an object of disgust. With a like purpose he admonished all by word and example to flee every danger threatening this virtue. Only when obedience required it, would he associate with persons of the other sex. He was wont to say: "It is a dangerous thing to associate with women, who but harm him who wishes to belong to God. One must avoid them and associate with them only when obedience demands."

God rewarded his spotless purity by granting him the power to free those who were molested by temptations against chastity,— at times by the use of some object, at other times by mere words. A youth who was suffering from a very grievous temptation was freed on girding himself with the girdle of the saint. A Turk who had been recently converted to the Catholic faith complained to the saint of more vehement temptations than he had ever had before. Joseph replied that this was due to the fact that formerly his false religion had not forbidden impurity and that the devil does not strive to secure control of what he already possesses. From that time on the man felt freed from these temptations and confirmed in the Catholic faith.

The most certain and miraculous evidence, however, of the saint's angelical purity was this, that he perceived a stench emanating from the bodies of incontinent persons, and that his own body exhaled an exceedingly pleasant odor which was noticed by others. On seeing a licentious person he recognized him as such by this stench. Once he appeared restless and perplexed, and, on being asked what ailed him, replied that he had just spoken with a licentious person, who had filled his nose with such a stench that he could not remove it, not even by using snuff. To fill others with a horror of the vice of impurity, he was wont to say that the impure stank before God, before the angels and men.

"The best proof of Joseph's purity," said Cardinal Brancati, "was given to all those who associated with him or only touched an object belonging to him; for there emanated from him a most pleasant perfume, which clung for a long time to all things he used. Even the rooms through which he passed long retained this unusual odor, and to find the way he had gone, it sufficed to follow this odor." [1]   This perfume which he diffused was regarded by all as supernatural; for it could be compared to no other perfume than that which emanated from a breviary of St. Clare, preserved in Assisi, and that of the shrine in which the remains of St. Antony are laid to rest and which those who have perceived it have called a fragrance from Paradise.

Our saint excelled in religious poverty. Although religious are permitted the use of many articles of food and clothing, yet he wished to be bereft not only of all superfluities, but even of most necessaries of life. His habit was ever the worst he could secure, and under it he wore a rough undergarment which better deserved the name of a cilice than of a garment. His small clothes were of rough linen. He never dressed

[1] Nuti devotes an entire chapter (41) to this subject.— Some instances of this "odor of sanctity" have been collected by Goerres, Mystik, vol. II, pp. 39–44; two recent instances are given in the biographies of Mary Agnes Clara Steiner (d. 1862) and Gemma Galgani (d. 1903).

otherwise, not even as a protection in the cold season, and put on slippers only when he appeared
in public. If questioned, on arriving at a monastery, whether he had brought his clothes with
him, he replied that he had certainly done so,
referring to the clothes he wore. In his last illness he consented to take two white handker-
chiefs at the insistence of the surgeon, but when
he saw they were made of linen, he said, " They
are too fine," and returned them, taking in their
stead others of coarser material.

His poverty in all other regards was of the
same heroic mold. He ate but once a day, and
then only a few herbs and vegetables, seldom
fish. Several times, when commanded to do so,
he ate meat, but, as already mentioned, his stomach always rejected it. He ate alone in his cell,
lest his frequent ecstasies cause disturbance in the
refectory; and after meals insisted on the removal
of even the smallest remnants of food. The
furniture of his cell consisted of a priedieu, two
cane chairs, a small table and several paper pic-
tures of saints. His bed was made up of several
boards and a pallet of straw. This uncom-
fortable and poor bed was so dear to him that
once, when he was commanded to use a mattress

and linen sheets because of illness, he could not bear this unwonted comfort, but said he felt as if all his bones were crushed. In order to satisfy him, his superior allowed him to use his dear boards again.

The saint had a great aversion to money. He always refused it, and when importuned to take it for the benefit of the monastery, would request the donors to bring it to the superior. He loathed it so much that one day, when several pious persons had secretly put a silver coin into his cowl, he began to breathe heavily and perspired as if he bore a great weight, and finally exclaimed, " I can bear it no longer." Not until the money had been removed was he again at ease. For the rest, he esteemed himself rich, and with joyful countenance would say that he had nothing, but God provided him with all things. He looked upon God as the source of all good and frequently repeated the words of his Seraphic Father, " My God and my all." When, on his deathbed, he was asked to make the customary renunciation and to give a list of the things he had in use, he could say to his superior, " Father Guardian, I would gladly make the renunciation, but I have nothing to renounce."

It may be said of our saint that he was wholly subject to his superiors. He frequently said he would rather die than disobey. He revered his superior as if he were St. Francis himself, and would not see any defect in him in order that he might not find even a shadow of a reason to disobey. To each superior he disclosed his manner of life and stated his readiness to change it if so directed. He did not wish to do aught without the merit of obedience, so that without the consent of the lay-brother, his companion, he would not even open or close the window of his cell. One day, while Extreme Unction was being administered to Father Caravaggio, his confessor, who was very sick and given up by the doctors, Joseph was enraptured and lifted up over the bed of the sick priest. On returning to himself, he wished to go back to his cell, but on hearing his superior command him to stay, he remained immovable at the place where he stood, not daring to take a step till the superior had given him permission. If commanded to do so, he ate meat, left his cell, spoke to persons, allowed his feet to be kissed, gave to his admirers any object he was using, although he had a great aversion to whatever redounded to his own honor and praise. Once his superior commanded him to eat a confection, and he ate it quickly. When asked by a religious how it had tasted, since he was accustomed to fast on bread and water, he quietly replied, " I merely obeyed." At another time the Father General commanded a religious to take away Joseph's old habit in order to give it to the Princess of Savoy, who had a great devotion toward the saint and had provided a new habit for him. At first, Joseph, not knowing of the command of his superior, objected, but as soon as he learned of it he quickly took off his cowl and habit saying, " If obedience requires it, I am satisfied that you take not only my habit, but also my skin and flesh." On another occasion he said, " If commanded to do so, I would not fear to enter a fiery furnace and would trust to be preserved uninjured because of the merit of obedience."

To induce others to love and practice obedience he extolled its merits and called it a " knife that kills the will of man and sacrifices it to God, a carriage that conveys a man comfortably to heaven, a little dog that leads the blind." " O holy obedience," he often exclaimed, " God Himself esteems thee." When enraptured, neither

blows nor the application of fire could recall him
to his senses, but if obedience called, he returned
forthwith. On being asked one day to explain
this, he replied that he did not hear the voice of
his superior when enraptured, but because God
loved obedience so well, and desired that he should
obey without delay, He made the vision disappear
at once. We have already recorded the words
of the saint, that God drew aside a veil before
the enraptured soul and showed it, as in a gallery, many beautiful and ineffable objects. Referring to this comparison he added that, at the
word of obedience, the Lord again drew the veil
and left the soul free to its duties.

The merit of his obedience was so great that
by it he obtained the power to terrify the devil
and subject even irrational animals to his will.
When, at the behest of his superior, he exorcised
persons possessed by evil spirits, he would command Satan to depart from their bodies by saying,
" Out of obedience I have come, therefore you
must depart." At times, after praying the Litany
of the Blessed Virgin, he would gently say: " I
have come, not to drive you from this body, but
only to obey; if, therefore, you wish to leave, do
so; but if not, do as you like; for me it is sufficient

to have obeyed." In this manner he confounded the proud spirit and forced him to leave his victim. Yet another means Joseph employed. During the exorcism of a possessed woman, the devil struck him a terrific blow in the face. The saint was not alarmed, but, kneeling down, drew forth the written command of his superior, gave it to the possessed person and said, " Here, take it! O holy obedience." He then prayed the Litany of our Lady, and the devil, unable to bear this child-like obedience, departed at once.

It was amazing with what alacrity irrational animals did the saint's bidding. A linnet, to which he often said, " Praise God," would praise the Lord or cease to do so at his command. Once, on setting free a gold-finch, he said to it : " Go, enjoy what God has given thee ; as for me I require nothing more of thee than that thou return when I call thee to praise with me thy God and mine." Obedient to these words, the bird flew about in the garden near by and, when Joseph called it, straightway came to praise the Creator. A hawk once killed a finch, which the saint had trained to say, " Jesus and Mary. Friar Joseph, pray your Breviary." The hawk returned at the saint's command and, when he reproached it saying, " Thou, thief, hast killed my finch and deservest that I should kill thee," it remained perched on the cage as if sorry for its misdeed, allowed Joseph to strike it with his hand, and only flew away when he said, " Now go. This time I will pardon thee, but do not do such a thing again."

A ram which had gone mad because bitten by mad dogs, was confined in a garden so as to harm nobody. The servant of God, accidentally coming to the place, was warned to beware of the animal. With a smile he replied that he trusted in God. He then turned to the ram, stroked it and said, " Foolish one, what dost thou here? Return to thy flock." On being freed, it hastened back to its flock, well and tame.

To the nuns of St. Clare at Copertino the saint presented a white lamb to watch over the discipline of the community. The lamb was always first in all exercises, abstemious, quiet in the chapel and ever alert to wake the sleepy by butting and jostling or to remove with hoofs and teeth any vain finery which it observed. When the lamb had died, the saint promised to send the nuns a bird which should prompt them to love God, and thus it came to pass. One day as the nuns were reciting the Divine Office, a forest songster perched on the window of the choir and sang most sweetly. And thus day by day the merry warble of the feathered songster accompanied and encouraged the chanting of the nuns, until one day it saw two novices quarrelling and flew between them in an endeavor to part them with its outspread wings and tiny claws. One of the novices struck the bird, and it flew away and did not return, though it had been with the community for five years. The nuns were grieved because of this and complained to Joseph, but he said: "It serves you right; why did you provoke it and chase it away? It is unwilling to come again." But, at their urgent request, he promised to send the bird again. At the first summons to choir, the bird not only came to the window and sang, but, grown more tame than before, flew into the monastery. The nuns tied a small bell to its foot. When it failed to appear on Holy Thursday and Good Friday, they again had recourse to Joseph, who replied to them: "I sent you the bird that it should sing, not that it should ring a bell. It has stayed away because during these days it has guarded the holy sepulchre. I will see that it comes back again." And the bird returned and remained a long time with the pious nuns.

The saint commanded two hares near the convent at Grottella, saying, " Go not too far from the church of our Lady; for there are many hunters lying in wait for you." They obeyed and profited by their obedience; for when hunters pursued the one, it fled into the church and thence into the monastery, where it leaped into the arms of Joseph. The saint said to it, " Did I not tell you not to go too far from the church, lest it cost you your skin? " The saint protected the hare from the hunters. The other rabbit, which was chased by dogs and concealed itself beneath Joseph's habit, had a like good fortune. When the Marquis of Copertino, who had arranged the hunt, came up and asked the saint whether he had seen the rabbit, he replied, " See, here it is, but do it no harm." The saint then said to the animal, " Go, jump into those bushes and remain there without moving." The hare obeyed and the dogs did not pursue it, to the great amazement of the Marquis and his whole party.

CHAPTER VII

IN HIS LIFE HE DID GREAT WONDERS
(ECCLI. 48, 15)

As has been recounted above, Joseph was not well talented; he had only sufficient knowledge of Latin to use the Breviary and the Missal.[1] God, however, bestowed on him a measure of wisdom which amazed even learned theologians. He penetrated deeply into the meaning of Holy Scripture, especially of the Psalms, and would say, " No better spiritual book can be found than the Breviary; to me it is the source of all profit." When asked regarding the more difficult mysteries, for example, the Most Blessed Trinity, the Incarnation, predestination, the efficacy of grace, justification, and similar subjects, he would reply readily with great erudition and would solve the difficulties proposed by very learned men. On such occasions he made use of comparisons from

[1] Gattari, 40.

the material world and explained all questions
with such lucidity that he soon convinced his
hearers. Of the many and learned religious who
questioned him, one admitted, " He knows more
than I." Another said, " Now I am learning a
new and more excellent theology." A third as-
serted, " My conversations with Father Joseph
have been of greater use to me than many years
of study." A fourth declared, " Joseph speaks
more profoundly on theological subjects than the
foremost theologians of the world." All agreed
that " the gifts of the Holy Ghost, wisdom,
science and intellect were made manifest in
Joseph."

To this heavenly light of wisdom was added
another, by means of which Joseph knew the
thoughts and secrets of others. When anyone
stained with sin came to him, he said, " Go
wash your face which you have sullied with ink,"
or, " Adjust your bow," referring to the person's
guilty conscience. If such a person replied, he
was not conscious of any particular sin, Joseph
would add the time, place and circumstances of
the sin. On the return of such a person after
confession, he kindly said, " Now all is well again
with you." He even knew the guilty ones with-

out seeing them.   Once he said to one who rapped at his door, " Go first to confession, then come again and enter."

Similar occurrences are recorded of him as a confessor.   A woman made her confession and added that she knew of no other sin.   But the saint replied, " Confess those evil thoughts to which you consented," naming the occasion and place.   The woman thereupon confessed that it had indeed been so.   In like manner he said to a novice, whom he had advised to write his general confession, " My son, here you have not expressed yourself well; for it was not as you have written here, but thus and thus."   On one occasion he revealed in a discourse to the novices their most hidden faults, so that all were greatly amazed.

If anyone prayed the Divine Office, the Litany or rosary with him, Father Joseph called attention to any distractions the person entertained.   To one he said, " Remain here," thus referring to his wandering thoughts.   To another he said, " You have prayed the Our Father very distractedly."   Another, who had not yet prayed the Office for the day, was asked at nightfall by the saint, " Where is the Divine Office?   The Breviary cries out against you."   It is related that people who had not a clear conscience or were slaves to passion, dreaded to meet him.

As he disclosed faults, so, too, he often revealed to others their good works and anxieties. Thus, he thanked a lady named Elizabeth, whom he met coming from church, for a " Salve Regina " which she had prayed for him. To a Tertiary who feared to reveal to him some doubts which troubled her, he said, " Why do you fear? Tell me your difficulties." Without allowing her to speak, he then revealed to her all she had wished to say to him. On another occasion he said to the same person: " Yesterday you scourged yourself and practised one other mortification. You entertained this thought. In future you must do this and omit that." He revealed to Cardinal Rapaccioli, Bishop of Terni, the good works he had done while in his room. Another time, when the Cardinal was much disturbed by doubts and was about to send a letter to Joseph explaining them, he received a letter from the saint in which, to his amazement, he found his doubts solved in detail. In like manner a religious received of Joseph, through a companion, advice regarding several matters about which he intended to consult him. To another, who was

very sad that he had not entered a stricter Order,
Joseph cheerily said: " What is the matter?
Why are you sad? Can you not practise what
the Reformati do? Be satisfied in the Order in
which you have taken vows."

Even hidden thoughts were revealed to the servant of God. He gently reproved a novice who,
during Terce, had thought of the fruit in the
garden, by repeating verbally to him what he had
said to himself, namely, " Today I shall climb the
fig-tree and eat my fill." A lay-brother who was
his companion on a journey and carried a gold-
finch, thought of different persons to whom the
saint might wish to present the bird. Joseph
suddenly turned to him and said, " Not to any of
the persons of whom you have thought, will I give
the bird, but I will set it free." He thereupon
opened the cage and let the bird fly.

Distance was no bar to his knowledge. One
night while Joseph was at prayer in the church
at Grottella, a lady who suffered severe pain sent
her servant to request the saint to come. Before
the man could deliver his message, the saint said,
" Son, go home; the pain has ceased, and your
lady is well."

One evening when speaking with the Guardian,

he suddenly exclaimed, "Oh, what a stench! Oh, what a hellish stench!" The Guardian noticed nothing; but Joseph, knowing the cause of the stench he perceived, obtained permission, hurried as fast as he could to Copertino, went directly to a certain house and rapped at the door till he was admitted. He then ran up the steps and came upon a number of sorcerers, men and women, with salves and oils in vases and in pots on the fire. In holy indignation he broke the vases into fragments with his cane, while his countenance appeared so terrible that the guilty ones fled in dismay.

The saint revealed the recovery of persons who lay sick at Rome, and the death of others, notably Popes Urban VIII and Innocent X, who died at the time he had foretold. Many other instances of his knowledge of things that had happened long before or at a great distance, could be adduced on sworn testimony of trustworthy witnesses.

The saint foretold the events of his own life even to the minutest details. His prophecies regarding others are very numerous; we will, however, content ourselves with narrating a few. A mother brought to him her two sons, that he might bless them before they set out for Rome, where they meant to study for the degree of doctor. " What," said the saint, " doctors? Yes, doctors in heaven." The two died soon after. A noble Polish youth asked him whether it were better for him to marry or to take orders, and received the answer, " Neither the one nor the other." A few months later the youth died. A sick man commended himself to the saint, that he might recover so as to provide for his wife and parents. The saint rejoined: " Why do you think of wife, of father and mother? You need patience, my son, for God wishes to take you to Himself. O Paradise, how beautiful is Paradise! " His prophecy was fulfilled in all its details; for the sick man recovered but died a sudden death within a month. In like manner Joseph foresaw the circumstances of the death of many others and the recovery of the sick.

Once, on seeing a vain courtesan, he said to the bystanders, " Behold, a Magdalen." He then turned to her and said, " God calls thee. Leave this vain finery and love God, thou Magdalen." She obeyed this summons of grace and after her conversion took the name Magdalen.

Two prophecies regarding a notary public came

true. Because he had not heeded Joseph's words, this notary was subjected to suffering, which the saint had foretold. He then entered the clerical state, but without the hope of becoming a priest because his father had left him no fortune. Joseph, however, said to him, " Be of good cheer; when the time comes, God will provide for you." And, indeed, he received the needed patrimony from a person of whom he had least expected it.

When Portolongone [2] was besieged by the King of Spain, in 1649, our saint foretold that the city would fall on the feast of the Assumption, as indeed happened. A doctor at Assisi had often commended himself to Joseph's prayers, asking that a son might be born to him. When his wife was near death in travail, the physician hastened to the saint to implore his prayer, but the latter reassured him by saying that the lady's life was not in danger. After the doctor had gone, Joseph smilingly said to a fellow-religious, " To-night a son will be born to the doctor; I did not wish to reveal it to him, lest it be said that I pose as a prophet." His words came true.

A marriage was the occasion of several remarkable prophecies. The saint sent congratulations

[2] On the island of Elba, taken by the French in 1646.

to the father of a young lady because of a pro-
jected alliance. The man thanked him for the
civility but answered that, owing to the great
social inequality between the persons in question,
the realization of his wish was far distant.
Thereupon Joseph said with a smile: " But what
if her husband is already born. The marriage
was made in heaven and will be contracted on
earth." The marriage took place. The mother
of the bride, fearing that witchcraft might have
influenced the transaction, sent to Joseph request-
ing him to say Mass for her intention, but without making known her suspicion. The servant of
God sent her word that she should not fear and,
because he was sick, have the Mass said by her
pastor. The marriage might then take place
without delay, and in time a son would be born
to those about to wed. The woman, astonished
and full of joy, especially because of the promised
son, requested that Joseph stand sponsor for the
boy. The saint, however, replied that she should
make a better choice because he would no longer
be among the living. All the words of the saint
were verified.

To a brave young man who was preparing to
go to war, Joseph foretold that he would not go;

thus it came to pass. A religious who was destined for the Congo mission was told by the saint that he would not go to the mission, as indeed happened. Another religious was commanded to go to Perugia to study, but Joseph remarked to him, " One is well off at Urbino, too." The friar went to Urbino and not to Perugia. Joseph said to Father Raphael Palma, Custos of the monastery at Assisi, " Oh, what a handsome head! How well the mitre will grace it! " The priest became a bishop. The dignity of the Cardinalate he prophesied to Nicholas Albergati (who later took the name Louis), to Antony Bichi, Bishop of Osimo, and to Father Lawrence Brancati of Lauria. All three received the sacred purple. The saint foretold to John Casimir, who later became King of Poland, his elevation to the throne. To Cardinal Benedict Odescalchi (later Pope Innocent XI), who much desired the arrival of a supply of grain to prevent a scarcity in Ferrara, where he was Legate, he foretold its early arrival. The two Custodes at Assisi were cheered by Joseph's promise that the need of their monastery would soon be relieved, and they received abundant help. A religious requested a favor of the newly elected Father General. The saint prophesied that he would receive it, but not until many years later, and from another General; thus it came to pass. In short, whatever Joseph foretold came true to the smallest detail.

Joseph was frequently honored by heavenly visions. Saints [3] appeared to him and conversed with him about Paradise. Angels, in visible form, brought him heavenly comfort. Jesus Christ appeared to him in the form of a tender child, in the consecrated host and on other occasions, nestled in his arms and by sweet words and fond caresses filled him with ineffable delight.

God revealed some of these favors to other souls. Sister Catharine of Cantu, a Tertiary, saw Joseph enter Assisi accompanied by two angels. To Sister Cecilia Nobili of Nocera [4] it was revealed that Joseph's guardian angel was of a higher angelic choir than those of ordinary men. The saint had such a great reverence for his guardian angel that he never entered his cell without inviting the angel to enter first. The same venerable servant of God, Sister Cecilia, saw the soul of Joseph take refuge in the wound of

[3] St. Bonaventure, St. Philip Neri, St. Felix of Cantalice.
[4] Gattari, 60.— Sister Cecilia died in the odor of sanctity, July 24, 1655.

the side of Christ; and at another time she saw his soul on the top of a very high mountain, which signified the mountain of perfection.

More than by such testimony of pious souls Joseph's sanctity was attested by the devil, the greatest enemy of all holiness. Thus Satan said to a religious who was exorcising him and who bound a girdle, which the saint had blessed, about the possessed one: "If you knew the virtue of this friar and how pleasing his soul is to God, you would be astonished. I must acknowledge this because God forces me to speak. Friar Joseph is the worst foe we have."

The infernal spirits treated Joseph as their enemy. One night the servant of God was standing before the altar of St. Francis, in the Basilica at Assisi, when he heard the door opened violently and saw a man enter, who advanced so noisily that his feet seemed cased in iron. The saint regarded him closely and saw that, as he approached, the lamps went out, one by one, till finally all were extinguished and the intruder stood at his side in utter darkness. Thereupon the devil, for he it was, furiously attacked Joseph, threw him on the floor, and attempted to strangle him. Joseph, however, invoked St. Francis, and saw him come forth from his tomb and relight with a small candle all the lamps, at the gleam of which the fiend suddenly vanished. By reason of this occurrence Joseph gave St. Francis the name " Lamplighter of the Church."

The devil made other attempts on the life of Joseph, by throwing him into a rapid stream in order to drown him, by taking hold of him to tear him to pieces, and by endeavoring to run him through with a sword, but all to no purpose. Though the evil one did succeed in striking him so terribly that his fellow-religious were horrified by the noise of the many blows and the rattling of chains, he did not succeed in tiring the patience of the saint. When asked by his fellow-religious as to the cause of the strange noises in his cell at night, Joseph laughingly replied, " It was only fun." All the devil accomplished by his implacable hatred was to give unmistakable proof of Joseph's sanctity.

Our saint frequently wrought miracles. We have already mentioned some and shall now relate a few others of the many that are on record.

In the hands of Joseph, or at his word, bread, wine, honey and other similar things were multiplied. The lame and the crippled he cured by

giving them a crucifix to kiss. He restored sight
to the blind by the touch of his hand, by placing
on their heads his biretta [5] or something he had
written. By the sign of the cross he healed
many of the fever and even recalled the dying to
life.

A nobleman of Naples once entered the cell of
Father Joseph and insolently said: " Impious
hypocrite, it is not your person, but the religious
garb you wear, which I respect and to it I trust,
that if you will make the sign of the cross over
my wound, it will heal." He then uncovered the
wound. Joseph smiled and replied with joyful
and humble mien, " What you say is true." He
blessed the wound, and it healed immediately.

The rare gift of bilocation (being at two places
at the same time) was given to our saint on two
occasions. There lived at Copertino an old man,
Octavius Piccinno, who was generally called
" Father." He had requested the saint, while
living at Grottella, to assist him in the hour of
death. The saint had promised to do so, and
added, " I shall assist you even though I should

[5] " Unlike the Friars Minor and the Capuchins, the Conventuals wear birettas and shoes." (Catholic Encyclope-
dia, IV. 346.)

be in Rome." This promise was a prophecy, and
its fulfilment involved a miracle. Joseph was at
Rome when the old man fell sick, but at the ap-
proach of his last hour hastened to assist him.
He was seen by many witnesses, especially by
Sister Teresa Fatali of the Third Order, who on
this occasion spoke to him and in amazement
asked, " Father Joseph, how did you come? "
He replied, " I came to assist the soul of
' Father,' " and then suddenly disappeared.

While living at Assisi, he was seen at Copertino assisting his mother in the hour of death.
She had much desired to see him and cried out
in sorrow, " Alas, my dear Joseph, I shall not see
you again." Presently a bright light filled the
room, and the dying woman, on seeing her son,
joyfully exclaimed, " O Father Joseph! O my
son! " At the same time the Father Custos at
Assisi met Joseph, sad and in tears, about to enter
the church. The Father Custos enquired as to
the cause of his sadness. With a sob, Joseph replied, " My poor mother has just died." Events
proved the truth of his words; for a letter from
Copertino soon brought the sad news. Several
persons, who lived with his mother and who
later came to Osimo, solemnly testified that the

saint had assisted his mother on her deathbed.

A very amazing miracle was wrought by our saint at Copertino. A flock of sheep had been killed by enormously large hailstones, and the shepherds begged the saint to help them. Joseph hurried out into the field, lifted up his heart to God, and then raised the animals, one by one, from the ground, saying, " In the name of God, arise! " All the animals arose, and the shepherds were so amazed that they could not utter a word to thank their benefactor.

CHAPTER VIII

One need not marvel that a man of such great
virtue and enriched with such gifts, attracted men
and aroused in all the desire to rank him among
their number, as did the Archconfraternity of St.
Antony of Padua at Rome and the Confraternity of St. Stephen at Assisi. Everyone esteemed it a privilege to know him and to associate
with him. His presence was so charming, his
words so gentle, and his company so pleasant,
that all were forced to love him. Many persons
of the highest rank came to visit him. He was
universally called " the holy friar " and esteemed
as such. Besides Cardinals Facchinetti, Ludo-
visi, Rapaccioli and Odescalchi, who have already
been mentioned, Cardinals Donghi, Pallotta,
Verospi, Paluzi, Sacchetti and others admired and
revered Father Joseph as a saint. On visiting
him, they were much edified by his virtues, his

holy words, his ecstasies and flights, and other wonderful gifts which they observed.

Prince Leopold of Tuscany, who was later created Cardinal, went to Assisi for the express purpose of making Joseph's acquaintance. While there, he had the good fortune of seeing him fall into ecstasy, with eyes fixed on a picture of the Mother of God, when the Father Custos said some words in praise of the Queen of Heaven.

The fame of Joseph's sanctity spread to Germany, France, Poland, and other countries, so that besides the Duke of Brunswick and the High Admiral of Castile, already mentioned, many other princes and lords came to Assisi to visit the holy man. Such visitors were the Duke of Bouillon from France, Isabelle, Duchess of Mantua, from Austria, Princes Radziwill and Lubomirski with their wives, Prince Zamoyski and other grandees from Poland. The royal Prince of Poland, John Casimir, visited the saint repeatedly. Joseph, on hearing of his wish to become a religious, advised him to enter the Society of Jesus in preference to any other Order, because he would be forced to leave the religious state, which he could not do if he entered any

other Order.[1]   On another occasion he advised
the Prince not to take sacred orders, and said
God would reveal His will to him explicitly.
John Casimir was raised to the Cardinalate by
Pope Innocent X, but after the death of his
brother Ladislaus was elected King of Poland.
Joseph, on seeing him at Assisi in a worldly
garb on his journey from Rome to his kingdom, smilingly said to him: " Did I not tell
you? Just go; for you will advance God's in-
terests more in this state of life than in the religious state."   On hearing this the King left,
well satisfied.   Knowing the great sanctity of
Joseph, he continued to consult him by letter and
received from him good counsel and even knowledge of future events in Poland.

A lady of rank who, prompted by curiosity,
had come with others to see the saint in ecstasy,
was put to shame.   When she entered and was
about to pronounce the holy names of Jesus and
Mary, as had been agreed upon, the saint reproached her with the words: " What! Should

---

[1] The saint doubtless had in mind that after the novitiate
the members of the Society of Jesus took " simple " vows,
whereas in other Orders " solemn " vows were taken after
the time of probation. Many theologians held that the
Pope could not dispense from " solemn " vows.

one come out of mere curiosity? Do you not know that God could work miracles on this wood? Go away in the name of God."

Mary, daughter of Charles Emmanuel of Savoy and Catharine of Austria, whom we have already mentioned, came to Assisi after having visited various sanctuaries of Italy. This princess, who had led a pious life from early youth and had been invested with the habit of the Third Order by Father Francis Angelus Cavallari, Guardian of the Conventuals at Turin, felt so drawn toward the saint that she was reluctant to leave Assisi. She therefore remained many days at Rivotorto, near Assisi, and then several months at Perugia, whence she returned repeatedly each week to discuss with Joseph the affairs of her soul and to spend whole days with him in holy converse. Her veneration grew in keeping with the miracles of which she was a witness and frequently the object.

The princess was somewhat deaf and used a silver ear-trumpet, but the voice of the saint she heard without the instrument and at some distance from him. She wrapped the saint's girdle about a finger, which she had bruised while closing a door, and at once felt free from pain.

She was frequently a witness of ecstasies and miraculous flights while assisting at Holy Mass said by the saint. Once she saw him, in his private chapel, hover three palms from the floor while elevating the Sacred Host. In the chapel of the Veil of Mary, whither she had brought a relic of the true cross encased in gold, she repeatedly saw him in ecstasy during Holy Mass. After Mass, when he had laid aside the vestments, she saw him fly upon the altar and remain there, with bent knees, in sweet ecstasy.

Once, when the princess was permitted to dine with the Father Custos and the saint in the sacristy of the upper church at Assisi, she witnessed an ecstasy. Joseph, out of obedience, consented to dine with the princess, but brought his own food, saying that he brought dinner to a poor pilgrim (meaning the princess). Hardly had they begun to eat, when the saint unexpectedly went into esctasy, fell on his knees with outspread arms and fixed his eyes on the princess. She felt great joy because of this and requested the Father Custos to recall him by virtue of obedience. At the word of his superior, Joseph came to himself and hurriedly went to his cell without saying aught else than his usual words in such cases, "Let my heart be undefiled in Thy justification, that I may not be confounded" (Ps. 118, 80). When asked by a religious regarding this occurrence, he replied, "We have two St. Clares; one still lives on earth, the other is in heaven," and added that he had seen such splendor on the countenance of the princess that he could not resist the impulse to kneel. Thus he did but praise her piety to conceal his own holiness.

CHAPTER IX

MY LIFE IS "HID WITH CHRIST IN GOD"
(COL. 3, 3)

(Antiphon to Magnificat of I. Vespers, Office of
St. Joseph)

In spite of the honors bestowed upon him, our
saint remained humble. From his lips no one
ever heard a word in his own praise. He habitually regarded himself as the least of all men and
called himself a "man dead and useless to all
purposes," or "brother ass," or the "most wicked
and infamous sinner among men." He once said
that if he had aught of good, it came from God,
who generally made use of the greatest sinners
to perform great things. On seeing people and
princes come to him, he said in astonishment, " I
know not why these people come to me; for I am
but an ignorant man and a poor sinner." After
a visit by persons of rank he would fall on his
knees, kiss the floor and repeat the words, " Not
to us, Lord, not to us, but to Thy name give

glory." (Ps. 113, 1.) He then repeatedly struck his breast and wept bitterly because of such visits.

The actions of the saint suited his words. He humbled himself not only before his superior, but before all his brethren, undertook with joy the lowliest tasks, detested all praise, and took pleasure in being insulted and despised. One day while the saint was in his cell, speaking to other religious on spiritual things, his confessor unexpectedly entered and, to try the saint's humility, scornfully said, " What did you say, hypocrite?" Joseph, without showing the least resentment, replied, " What you say is true," and then covered his face with both hands.

In his efforts to hide the gifts and graces he received from God, he ascribed the supernatural perfume which emanated from his person, to aromatic substances which he designedly carried about with him. It was ascertained, however, that the odor was present even if he carried nothing or even malodorous things about his person. His ecstasies and flights he called sleep, infirmity, frailty or physical weakness. Often, when he felt ecstatic impulses of love, he would say, in order to avoid the admiration of men, " Enough,

enough, cease, cease, no further," and begged God to deprive him entirely of such heavenly consolations.

He was wont to extol the virtue of humility and to admonish others to practise it. To the novices, in particular, he said: "Some of you will be called to preach, but be not elated because of that; for a preacher is like unto a trumpet which produces no tone unless one blows into it. Before preaching, pray to God, 'Thou art the spirit and I am but the trumpet, which, without Thy breath, can give no sound.'"

The following instance shows how he endeavored to humble himself. While at Copertino he went, upon command of his superior, to the house of a lady who was a member of the Third Order. While there, another Tertiary came on a visit with her child, about three years of age. Joseph caressed the child, placed it on a chair, and said, "Little one, repeat after me: 'Brother Joseph is a great sinner and, when he dies, he will go to hell'." But the child, hardly able to speak distinctly and unable to understand the meaning of the words, replied clearly and distinctly, "Brother Joseph is a great saint and, when he dies, he will go to Paradise." The saint rejoined

with seeming anger: " Will you not speak as I
prompt you? Now, say as I do, ' Brother Joseph
is a great sinner.' " But the child repeated his
former words, " Brother Joseph is a great saint."
Joseph, taking the child by the ears and hair,
said, " Will you not say as I do?" and again
prompted, " Brother Joseph is a great sinner
and, when he dies, he will go to hell." But the
child repeated a third time, " Brother Joseph is
a great saint, and, when he dies, he will go to
Paradise." Those present were touched unto
tears and convinced that God had wished, by the
mouth of an innocent child, to reward and exalt
Joseph because of his humility.

Pope Innocent X, on learning of Joseph's many
rare gifts and of the concourse of people who
went to Assisi to visit him, decided to remove him
in order to shield and preserve his sanctity. By
written order of the General Inquisition to the
Father Inquisitor at Perugia, Father Joseph was
transferred to the monastery of the Capuchins at
Pietrarubbia. This monastery was built on a
slope of Mount Carpegna, in the diocese of Mon-
tefeltro, Duchy of Urbino. The papal command
was executed July 23, 1653. Although Joseph,
by divine revelation, foresaw this trial, he mani-

fested some anxiety, because he wished to live
with his beloved fellow-religious near the tomb
of his Seraphic Father. In fact, he was so
frightened that the Father Custos had repeatedly
to reassure him.[1]   Obedience, however, prevailed
over his fears and, kissing the feet of the Father
Inquisitor, he hurried into the carriage which
stood ready.[2]   Tranquil of heart he undertook
the journey, even though he knew not his des-
tination.

The journey was an occasion for new manifestations of the saint's virtue. In a litter carried by two mules, which was substituted for the
carriage at Città di Castello,[3] he crossed ravines
and rocks without mishap, to the great astonishment of his companion. On his arrival at Pietrarubbia, he prostrated himself at the feet of the
Guardian, whom he recognized, though he had
never seen him before. This superior had received strict command from the Father Inquisitor to restrain Joseph from associating with
others than Capuchins and from corresponding

[1] Gattari, 63–64.

[2] In the haste of departure the saint forgot his Breviary, spectacles, mantle and hat (Montanari, 101).

[3] Montanari, 98.

THE SACRO CONVENTO AT ASSISI
Where St. Joseph lived, 1639–1653

with anyone. The saint was so perfectly obedient in all things that he took no step without the leave of the superior and never enquired as to the reasons for the restrictions to which he was subject.

At Pietrarubbia Joseph continued to practise mortification, patience, and every other virtue. At times he would weep bitterly over the sufferings of Jesus Christ. At other times he would joyfully sing his usual spiritual hymns, in which he occasionally invited the Capuchins to join. Here, too, he was favored by God with a knowledge of the secrets of others, with revelations of future events, with frequent miracles, with apparitions of angels and saints and of Jesus Christ Himself, and with continual ecstasies in his cell or in the garden, but especially at the altar.

The Inquisition intended that the saint should remain hidden in the solitary mountains. God, however, permitted him to become so widely known that the church could not hold the crowds which gathered to assist at his Mass.[4] Because of this some removed the roof, while others broke

[4] People came from Monte Feltro, Fossombrone, Fano, Pesaro, Aricium and Cesena (Daumer, 69).

openings into the wall of the church in order to see him. For greater convenience many built themselves huts near the monastery or even erected inns. The saint stayed three months at Pietrarubbia. Then command was given by Rome to the Archbishop of Urbino to remove him to the Capuchin monastery at Fossombrone. Mario Viviani,[5] Canon and Archpriest of the cathedral, was entrusted with the execution of the task.

Our saint, buoyed up by the thought that God is everywhere, undertook with joy this journey to Fossombrone. It was characterized by frequent ecstasies and miracles. A stubborn mule, attached to the saint's litter, and a horse used by one of the party,[6] which before had refused to bear any burden, were quiet and obeyed the voice of the guide during the journey. A violent shower, which annoyed the others very much, did not even moisten the saint's garments.

Although the greatest secrecy was observed, his arrival at the monastery of Fossombrone became known at once to the people. They came in throngs to the monastery, desirous to see the saint and to commend themselves to his prayers;

[5] Gattari, 72.   [6] Gattari, 73.

and they came in such numbers that, for fear of violence, the friars dared not go out, but concealed themselves within the convent. In spite of this concourse of people Joseph was dead to the world and isolated to such a degree that he said Mass at a private altar prepared for the purpose. Here was verified his reply to the Father Guardian, who had asked him one evening, when about to retire, " What are you doing here, Friar Joseph? " The saint had joyfully answered, " I am burying one who is dead." The solitude gave him so much greater freedom for God, with whom he conversed without interruption. The virtues of the saint most remarked during his stay at Fossombrone were charity toward the sick religious of the monastery and obedience. The saint did not even go down into the garden without special permission, although he was free to do so.

Of the many ecstasies which occurred at Fossombrone three deserve special mention. The first took place in the monastery garden when a Capuchin, in presence of the saint, spoke of the glories of Mary. Uttering his usual loud cry, the saint ran towards the speaker with outspread arms and with such impetuosity that both fell to the ground. The other Capuchins, hearing the noise, hastened thither and saw Joseph immovable and in ecstasy, in which condition he remained about an hour and a half.

The second rapture occurred in the same garden on the evening of the Sunday on which the gospel of the Good Shepherd is read. Joseph happened to see a lamb in the garden, and mounting as usual from created things to the contemplation of the supernatural, joyfully said, "Look, a lamb!" When he was about to take hold of it, a friar quickly lifted it and placed it in his arms. After petting the animal he took hold of its feet and placed it on his shoulders. Absorbed in contemplation of the Good Shepherd, he then began to run about the garden, saying with joy to the Guardian, "Father Guardian, see here the Good Shepherd, who brings back the lost sheep." Finally, he threw the lamb into the air and flew after it above the highest trees, where he remained enraptured, kneeling with outstretched arms for more than two hours, to the amazement of the religious.

The third ecstasy was experienced by the saint on Pentecost. When, during his Mass, he came to the words of the Sequence, "Veni, Sancte

Spiritus," the fire of divine love burst forth with such power in his breast that he tore himself from the altar and, with a noise like thunder and the speed of lightning, gyrated about the whole chapel with such impetuosity, that all cells of the dormitory shook and the terrified religious ran out from their rooms, crying, " An earthquake ! " But, on entering the chapel, they discovered the cause of the disturbance to have been the saint, whom they found in ecstasy and absorbed in contemplation of the Divine Comforter.

Joseph spent about three years at Fossombrone, with the exception of the few days of the provincial chapter, during which he was, by command of the Holy Office, transferred to the Capuchin monastery at Montevecchio. Here he lived with great joy, especially in consequence of a vision of the " dear old saint," as he called St. Felix.[7] After his return to Fossombrone, Christ appeared to him in the guise of a pilgrim and strengthened him. The Capuchins became attached to him and revered him because of the occurrences just related, the fulfilment of his prophecies and his insight into the thoughts and

[7] St. Felix of Cantalice, beatified 1625, canonized 1712 (Acta Sanctorum, l. c., 1039).

secrets of others. To a priest he revealed a temptation that had disturbed him at Mass. To a novice he said, " Son, you have a good mother; she blesses you daily with the sign of the cross." The novice later learned that his mother gave him this blessing each day from a balcony.[8] The religious were attached to him also on account of the holy admonitions which he gave them. One religious asked him, whether he knew that those who carried the rule of St. Francis about their person would be blessed by the Seraphic Father. Joseph replied, " I know it well, but it is far better to have the rule in one's heart than to carry it about." By reason of these and many other happenings, it was not surprising that these pious religious were grieved to learn that the saint was about to leave them.

[8] Gattari, 80.

CHAPTER X

A SAINT'S "PARADISE" (ST. JOSEPH)

On the accession of Pope Alexander VII, a delegation of eight Conventual Provincials [1] entreated his Holiness to restore Joseph to the Conventuals. The Holy Father enquired to which place they wished him to be sent. They replied, to the monastery at Assisi, where he had previously been. But the Pontiff was of the opinion that there was no dearth of holy religious at Assisi, which had always been a school of true religious discipline. Several days later he informed the superiors that he wished Joseph to be sent to the monastery at Osimo, an old city in the Marches, six hours distant from the sanctuary of Loreto. The Pope's nephew, Antony Bichi, was then Bishop of Osimo.

The Papal brief was dated 1656, but, owing to a pest then raging in parts of Italy, could be exe-

[1] Gattari, 83. This occurred in May, 1656 (Acta Sanctorum, 1008).

cuted only the following year, when the Secretary General of the Order was sent to take Joseph to Osimo. By divine revelation the saint knew all this, and also the hour of his departure. He, therefore, against his wont, opened his window and placed himself near it about half-past eight o'clock [2] of the evening of July 6, 1657. A lay-brother, his companion, surprised by this, asked him why he had done so. The saint replied, that he would leave the monastery in a few hours to return to his Order and that the Father Secretary, who was to take him back, was already near.

The Father Secretary arrived about half-past nine that evening,[3] laid before the Guardian the command of Rome and, to avoid delay, left with Joseph that same night. The pious religious, as a last mark of affection, accompanied Joseph some distance on the stony path leading to the road, and with tender care placed a sudarium on his breast and another on his back that he might come to no harm if, in descending the mountain, he should perspire. Before leaving them he gave back to them these cloths, which diffused a most

[2] "Un' ora di notte." This time is reckoned from sun-set.

[3] "Alle due ore di notte."

pleasant odor. This perfume was not only noticeable on the way, but, on their return, permeated the whole monastery.

The joy of the Conventuals at the return of Joseph was very great. He himself, though ever resigned to the will of God, was glad to return, and evinced his joy on arriving at the first monastery of his Order at St. Victoria delle Fratte. His guides, though familiar with the place, had lost the way in the dark and wandered about in the neighboring woods. The saint, who had never before been in the place, said to them, " Go yonder, where the moon is rising." They turned in that direction and soon saw the bell-tower of the church which adjoined the monastery.[4] After his arrival, Joseph learned that the monastery had been established and built by St. Francis himself and, prostrating himself, he kissed the floor and thanked God for allowing him to live again among his brethren and die in their midst.

The Bishop of Fossombrone and his domestics came that very night to receive the saint's blessing. This prelate detailed one of his servants to lead the saint's horse on the stony path during the following night, when the journey was con-

[4] Gattari, 86.

tinued. The better to perform his task, the servant held the bridle of the saint's horse with one hand and with the other a burning candle. Though a violent wind was blowing, the candle was not extinguished, nor did it seem to grow smaller, though it burned for several hours. The man ever after preserved the candle as a relic.

To avoid any concourse of people, the party avoided the cities and larger villages and stopped only at hamlets and farms. At one such farmhouse a poor woman complained to the saint that the melons from the sale of which she derived a livelihood for herself and family, were being destroyed by worms. Joseph, moved to pity, blessed the garden and that year it produced more and larger melons than ever before.

When the saint finally arrived at the walls of Osimo, he was obliged to wait till evening to enter the city. While he viewed the country side from the porch of a house, a priest showed him the cupola of the Holy House of Loreto. Joseph, on looking, suddenly exclaimed, "Do you not see the angels who ascend and descend from heaven to yonder Sanctuary?" Immediately after saying these words he uttered his usual cry and flew in ecstasy from the porch, which was twelve palms from the ground, to the foot of an almond tree, a distance of fifteen yards.[5]

On the evening of July 10, 1657, Joseph arrived at the monastery of the Conventuals at Osimo. A secluded room with a private chapel and a garden were assigned to him, and a brother given him as associate and servant. Pope Alexander VII had commanded this, that the saint might not be annoyed by the people. During the remainder of his life he had not the least intercourse with anyone except with the Bishop, his Vicar-General, the religious of the monastery, and, in case of need, with the doctor and surgeon. He left his room only to visit the sick religious of the monastery and once, at night, when all doors had been carefully locked, to look at the church. He was nevertheless contented in his seclusion and was wont to say, "I live in a city, yet it seems to me that I live in a forest, or, rather, in a paradise." In very truth he could call his new abode a paradise; for his soul was almost continually enraptured.

Heaven only knows of all the sweet ecstasies which here united him with God. Many, how-

[5] "Sei canne."— The "almond-tree of St. Joseph" is still an object of veneration (Gattari, 89).

ever, became known. Several were witnessed by
Cardinal Bichi, Bishop of Osimo. On one occasion he was sitting beside the saint and conversing
with him, when he saw him rise rapidly and, with
outstretched arms and open eyes, remain deprived
of the use of his senses, and though a gnat
crawled over the apple of his eye, he did not
move his eyelids in the least. At times the religious found him in his chapel wrapped in ecstasy, and would carry him like a corpse to his
room. Occasionally these raptures lasted for six
or seven hours. Once the friars saw him rise to
a height of three paces and press his face to that
of an image of the Infant Jesus, which stood
above the altar of his chapel. In his cell he
danced in delightful ecstasy with this same waxen
image of the Divine Child and pressed it to his
breast violently but without damaging it. On
Christmas he would invite all the friars to his
oratory, where he had erected a crib. He would
then sing songs he had composed in honor of
the Christ child and invariably fall into ecstasy.
He loved the Child Jesus much, and it is recorded
that Jesus appeared to him in the form of a child
at Osimo and at other places.

His life at Osimo was one of prayer. His

daily prayers included the Divine Office, the Little Office of our Lady, the Office of the Dead, the Office of the Cross, the Office of the Holy Ghost, the Seven Penitential Psalms with Prayers, the Litany of our Lady, and the Rosary.[6] What time remained was given to pious reading, edifying converse with his fellow-religious and enjoyment of heavenly delights when he celebrated Holy Mass. It was certainly marvellous that the saint always continued the Mass where he had broken off, and that during his many ecstatic flights, upwards and downwards, forwards and backwards, his garments were never disarranged.

Living for God alone, Joseph slept but a brief time on his bed of boards, and this unwillingly. He ate very little and only Lenten foods. He was satisfied with what was set before him and did not even say a word when his lay-brother neglected to bring him any food for two days. The devil did not cease to tempt and molest him in various ways. But the servant of God courageously said, " I do not fear his attacks; for I am with God and far from the world."

Although the saint lived in such seclusion that he had not visited the city of Osimo and knew

[6] These details are from Gattari, 92.

none of its citizens, yet he spoke of the city and its inhabitants, of their homes and their affairs, both public and private, as if he had seen all with his own eyes. The inhabitants of Osimo experienced many graces and miracles without knowing who wrought them. Sometimes the miracle was effected by a mere word. He quelled a threatening storm by the words, "Go away in God's name." At times he wrought miracles by means of objects which he used. By a girdle he had worn he freed a man from impure temptations. By like objects he cured such as suffered from earache, severe pains, dangerous fevers, hemorrhages or other infirmities.

The supernatural light by which Joseph knew secrets and foresaw the future, continually increased. This gift was especially remarked by his fellow-religious. To one of them he related even the smallest details of a journey he had made. Another friar he reminded of having forgotten to recite a promised prayer. One day, when a priest was called to the confessional, he revealed to him that one of his penitents, prompted by false shame, had concealed a sin in several confessions. "Go, kill the scorpion," said the saint. The Father confessor understood

these words on seeing a scorpion come forth
from the penitent after he had confessed the sin.
When several persons recommended to his
prayers a peasant's wife, who had been seriously
wounded, Father Joseph reassured them by saying, " She will not die."

By this same heavenly light the saint discovered that several religious had left the monastery
one evening during the carnival to enjoy themselves in the home of relatives. " Where are thy
sheep?" Joseph asked the Father Guardian, who
came to his room. These words were reported
to the friars and they quickly returned and entered the saint's cell. The servant of God was
so overjoyed at their return that he took hold of
one of them by the arm, lifted him with one hand
from the floor and whirled him about the cell, as
if he were but a straw. Thus did he show his
tender love towards his fellow-religious, whom
he regarded safe from all danger when in the
monastery.

CHAPTER XI

OBTAINING THE PRIZE (1 COR. 9, 24)

On entering the monastery at Osimo, Joseph had foretold that he would die there, saying, "This is my rest" (Ps. 131, 14). Speaking more clearly of his death he added that, if he were not the first, he should certainly be the second friar of Copertino to die at Osimo. Events proved him to be the second. He revealed the approach of his death to Father Sylvester Evangelisti on the return of the latter to Osimo from Montefiascone, where he had been two years.[1] With him the saint agreed that the one who should die first should be assisted by the other in death. On Father Sylvester's arrival at Osimo Joseph said to him, "Have you come at last? Why did you not wish to come? Did you not remember your promise to assist me in death?" Even the day of his death he foretold by saying to his brethren that he would die on the day on which he could not receive the immaculate flesh

[1] Gattari, 140.

of the Divine Lamb, meaning Holy Communion. Knowing that his end was near, he ardently desired the approach of the happy moment when he should be wholly united with God. This holy desire shone from his countenance and revealed itself in his words. It even caused him to loathe all food that might prolong his life.

August 10, 1663, he was seized with a fever. This filled him with great joy and he replied, to those who advised him to ask of God the gift of health, " No, God forbid! " The rigorous mode of life led by the saint had sapped his strength, weakened his stomach, and emaciated his body to such a degree that he could offer but feeble resistance to the fever. He lay down on his poor couch, resigning himself entirely to the will of the doctors and his superiors. For five days the fever was intermittent and he was able to rise each morning to say Holy Mass in his private oratory, where he experienced the usual delights of spirit in a higher degree than ever. He had miraculous ecstasies and flights especially during his last Mass, which he read on the feast of the Assumption.

When the violence of the fever no longer allowed him to celebrate the Divine Mysteries, he requested permission to assist at Holy Mass and to receive Holy Communion each morning. It was touching to see him glow with delight at Holy Communion; for on receiving the Blessed Sacrament he would exclaim, " Behold, my delight! " and thereupon would swoon away, closing his eyes and turning pale as a corpse. As the illness progressed, the flame of divine love in his heart grew so intense that it could no longer be confined, but frequently burst from his lips in the words, " O love, O love! " At the same time he would press his hands to his breast as if he would open it to give vent to the fire within. He would then turn to those who assisted him and admonish them to pray, or thank them for their kindness.

The surgeon marvelled much to see the servant of God, because of an ecstasy, insensible to the hot iron he applied to cure him. He marvelled even more when the saint revealed to him an old and secret sin which he himself had forgotten.

When no longer able to rise from his bed, because of the violence of the fever, the saint yet wished to receive Holy Communion daily. The last Communion, which he received as Viaticum on September 17, the day before his death, re-

vealed the degree and strength of his love.   On
hearing the sound of the bell that announced the
approach of his Beloved, he suddenly rose from
his bed and flew in rapture from the door of his
room to the stair above his chapel.   There on
his knees, with a supernatural light diffused about
his face, he received his hidden God.   After Holy
Communion he fell into a swoon, caused more by
love than weakness, and was carried back to his
bed.

At the beginning of his illness Joseph had said,
" The ass [meaning his body] begins to ascend
the mountain."   During its progress he remarked, " The ass has arrived half-way up the
mountain."   Finally he said, " The ass has
reached the summit of the mountain, he can no
longer move and will leave his hide here."   With
great fervor he often repeated the words, " I desire to be dissolved and to be with Christ " (Phil-
lip. 1, 23), or, " God be praised, God be thanked,
the will of God be done."

After receiving Extreme Unction he joyfully cried out, " Oh, what a pleasant odor!   Oh,
what a fragrance!   Oh, what a sweetness of paradise! "   He then requested that the profession of
faith be read, begged pardon of all for his faults,

and entreated that his body be interred, without
any solemnity, in some remote and hidden spot,
that nobody might know where Friar Joseph was
buried.   The Vicar General then asked the dying
saint to bless him and all present.   After receiving his blessing, the Vicar General told the saint
that he had been authorized by the Holy Father,
through Cardinal Ghigi, to give him the papal
blessing.   Joseph marvelled that the Vicar of
Christ was mindful of so lowly and worthless a
friar and replied, " That is not a favor which one
may receive in bed."   Although near death, he
rose and, supported by those present, went to his
oratory, where the Litany was recited and on his
knees and with great devotion he received the
papal blessing.   He was then hurried back to bed,
where he prepared for his last journey by repeated acts of love of God.

A religious, to cheer him, spoke to him of the
glories of Paradise.   The saint replied, " I do not
want to go to hell, because God is not praised
there."   Another said to him, " Friar Joseph, it
is now time to fight and conquer the devil!"
Joseph rejoined, " The victory shall not be want-
ing."   Nothing remained for him but the glori-

ous triumph, the approach of which he now beheld.

The saint felt uneasy, not because of pain, but as he himself said, as a consequence of his vehement love, which prompted him to use all efforts to free his soul from the bonds that still detained it. To Father Sylvester Evangelisti,[2] who spoke to him of this love, he said, " You understand it! You understand it! " He gave utterance to this love in the words which he addressed to the crucifix, " Take this heart, burn and rive this heart, my Jesus." To those who suggested to him ejaculatory prayers and mentioned the love of God, he said, " Say it once more."

After several ejaculations to his dear mother, as he called the Most Blessed Virgin Mary, and while the priest who assisted him prayed the " Ave Maris Stella," Joseph yielded up his soul to God, a sweet smile and bright light spreading over his countenance. The saint died shortly after midnight [3] following September 18, 1663.

[2] Gattari, 149.

[3] " Sulle cinqu' ore, e tre quarti della notte."— The Brief of Beatification designates the 19th as the day of death, " die decimanona Septembris."

He had attained an age of sixty years and three months and had spent the last six years, two months and eight days of his life at Osimo.

Joseph was tall and well built. His bearing was dignified, his gestures natural and unassuming. His features were somewhat homely, his eyes black and very vivacious and, because he habitually raised them to heaven, they gave him a peculiar charm and gravity. The expression of his countenance was always serene and, owing to his habitual recollection, serious and majestic. He wore a long, heavy beard which, originally black, turned gray in later life, as did also his hair. Though he spoke but little, his converse was cordial and animated and often characterized by a holy gaiety. The saint spent nearly half of his life away from his native country, yet he always spoke his native dialect with a singular charm.[4]

On opening the body of the saint for the purpose of embalming, it was found that the pericardium was shrivelled up, the ventricles of the heart without blood and the heart itself withered and dry. This was looked upon as an effect of the ardor of his love of God. The body was

[4] This description is given by Gattari, 151.

BODY OF ST. JOSEPH OF COPERTINO

washed with spirits and laid on a sheet. In some unknown way the sheet caught fire and the flames spread over the whole corpse. On extinguishing the flames it was found that the body was not harmed and that the beard and hair were not even singed.

The remains were carried to the sacristy and there laid out in state. A barrier of wood was erected around the bier, and twenty-four persons,— eight canons, eight noblemen, and eight religious of the monastery,— were detailed to guard the sacred remains. These precautions were necessary; for the people came in great numbers from the city and surrounding country and, crying as with one voice, " The holy priest who lived in the monastery of St. Francis is dead," they desired to see him after death whom they could not see during life. On the 19th of September all were allowed to enter the sacristy to view the remains; this continued till 9:15 in the evening. September 20th the obsequies were held, in which the Cathedral Chapter, the secular clergy, and all religious communities of the city took part. Till after eleven o'clock in the evening the body remained exposed to public veneration and was then placed in a coffin of wood to be buried next day. A renewed concourse and clamor of the people caused the coffin to be re-opened and the body exposed to view for an hour, after which the guards, by persuasion and force, induced the people to leave. The body was then taken from the temporary coffin and laid into another of cypress, and this was placed into a box of oak. Next day the remains were borne to the church and there buried in the chapel of the Immaculate Conception.

CHAPTER XII

THE "MEMORY OF AN ADMIRABLE SAINT"

(Clement XIV, Decree extending the Feast of St. Joseph to the Universal Church)

Owing to the many and striking miracles by which God glorified his servant Joseph after death, the informative inquiries were begun two years after his demise by authority of the Bishops of Nardo, Assisi, and Osimo. Pope Innocent XI appointed a commission for the introduction of the cause and authorized the Bishops of the aforesaid dioceses to conduct new inquiries by Apostolic authority. Under Clement XI the usual discussion was begun regarding the heroic degree of the theological and cardinal virtues of the saint. This process was brought to a favorable close under Clement XII, who on the feast of the Assumption of our Lady, 1735, made public the solemn decree asserting the heroic virtue of Joseph. The discussion of the miracles was then taken up. The first (antepreparatory) congregation was held March 2, 1751, the second (preparatory) on November 16th of the same year, the third (general) congregation on the anniversary of the saint's death, September 19, 1752. On the feast of St. Francis, October 4, 1752, Pope Benedict XIV published the solemn decree of approbation of two miracles, by which it had pleased God to glorify the dwelling and the tomb of the saint.

These miracles were the following. A swelling had formed on the right knee of Victor Mattei of Osimo and had grown in the course of six years to such an extent that it was finally as large as a loaf of bread and very hard. It was impossible for him to kneel or to walk freely, and he was tortured with incessant pain, which, about a month before his cure, became almost unbearable. The surgeon who was called, realizing that the malady was chronic and that by an incision the sick man would be exposed to great danger, refused to undertake an operation. About the time Mattei despaired of all human aid, the death of Joseph took place. As a last resort the sick man took refuge to supernatural means, trusting to be healed by God because of the merits of the saint, the fame of whose holiness had already spread. On the morning of September 19th, he dragged himself to the church of St. Francis. The body of the saint lay in state in the sacristy and, not being able to come near because of the great crowd, Victor obtained permission to go to the room in the monastery in which Father Joseph had lived. He devoutly entered and at length came to the private chapel, where the saint had said Holy Mass. He there made an act of lively faith and pressed his knee against the step of the altar which was worn down by the knees of the saint during his long protracted prayers. On touching the step all pain and the swelling disappeared at once, so that no trace of the infirmity remained. The knee was perfectly healed and could be moved like the other, which had never been affected.

The other miracle was wrought on Stephen Mattei, the twelve year old son of the above mentioned Victor Mattei, in November of the same year, 1663. While throwing stones at play with other boys, he was struck in the right eye. The cornea and uveous coat were cut and humor mixed with blood ran out. The whole eye appeared to be crushed and pressed into its socket. The doctor and surgeon, seeing that the sight of

the eye could not be restored, endeavored during
several days to heal the wound and form a scar.
The boy was exhorted by his mother to trust in
the aid of Father Joseph, by whose miraculous
power his father had been healed two months
before. He had recourse to the saint, first by
prayer at home, and then, accompanied by his
mother, at the saint's grave. Here mother and
son knelt and devoutly repeated their prayer.
The boy then pressed his blind eye to the stone
that covered the saint's grave and instantly recovered his sight.

Pope Benedict XIV published the decree of
approbation of these two miracles on the feast of
St. Francis after having said Mass at the altar
of this saint in the Basilica of the Twelve Holy
Apostles. At the solicitation of the General of
the Order, Father Charles Antony Calvi, and
because of the favorable report and opinion of
the illustrious Louis Valenti, who was Promotor
Fidei, it pleased his Holiness to grant a dispensa-
tion from the general congregation. This is
otherwise held after approbation of the virtues
and miracles to determine whether it be safe to
proceed with the solemnities of Beatification. A
papal rescript was therefore published, December

12, 1752, stating that, after the approbation of the miracles and virtues, and in consideration of the special circumstances of the case, beatification might be proceeded to without a new congregation. On the feast of St. Matthias, February 24, 1753, the servant of God, Joseph of Copertino, was solemnly beatified by his Holiness, Benedict XIV, in the Vatican Basilica, amid the rejoicings of a great concourse of people.

The miracles wrought through the intercession of Blessed Joseph of Copertino continued, so that Bishops and princes, together with the Conventuals, entreated Rome to take up the cause of his canonization. July 17, 1754, the Holy Father approved of the resumption of the cause and by Apostolic authority three miracles were investigated. Pope Clement XIII approved the finding of the Congregation of Rites as to the validity of the process, March 7, 1761. Two congregations, September 18, 1764, and December 10, 1765, found the processes to be valid and the three miracles authentic. In the general congregation of September 22, 1766, his Holiness ordained that public prayers be offered to implore the divine guidance, and on October 12th following, he published the decree establishing the authenticity of the new miracles. In the following general congregation it was unanimously decided that canonization could safely be proceeded with. A decree to this effect was published soon after, and on July 16, 1767, Pope Clement XIII promulgated in the Vatican Basilica the Decree placing Blessed Joseph in the list of Saints.

A brief narration of the three miracles investigated will form a fitting close to an account of a life so full of the miraculous.

Magdalen Panzironi was afflicted with an abdominal tumor. This growth was large and hard as stone, and gradually robbed her of all strength. Fever, headache, and other symptoms set in, so that she was confined to her bed, and towards the end of October, 1753, her dissolution seemed near at hand. She could not speak, her body grew cold, and the doctors regarded the case as hopeless. She received Extreme Unction on the 31st of October, and her demise was looked upon as so certain that the servants had begun to sew her shroud. In this extremity her niece exhorted the dying woman to invoke Blessed Joseph and place her trust in him. She then brought a relic of the saint from an adjoining room and pressed it into the hand of Magdalen; at the same time another woman laid a picture of the saint above the tumor.   Instantly Magdalen opened her eyes and, declaring herself fully restored, arose.   The doctors, who returned within an hour, could find no trace of the tumor. Magdalen partook of the evening meal with the family, went to church next morning, and was able to attend to all her domestic duties.

Benedicta Pierangelini was afflicted at the age of thirty-two (1741) with palpitation of the heart and difficulty in breathing.   This she bore in silence for eight years, but in 1749, frequent paroxysms of a severe nature forced her to consult physicians.   They discovered a growth in the cardiac vessels which interfered with the circulation of the blood.   During the six years following she remained under medical care.   The only remedy the doctors could apply was bloodletting.   This remedy was resorted to repeatedly each week and, at times, was applied more than once the same day.   In January, 1756, she received the last Sacraments.   On the 18th, when death seemed at hand, her sister prompted her to have recourse to Blessed Joseph of Copertino and laid a relic of the saint on her breast.   The bystanders then prayed an Our Father and a

Hail Mary in honor of the saint.   A paroxysm,
more severe than any preceding one, shook the
woman, and the doctor, feeling prompted to do
so, applied his lancet to her right arm.   With
the blood there came forth two growths and fell
into the vessel of water, which was placed to receive the blood.   One growth was about an inch
in length, the other of the size and shape of a
pigeon's egg.   At the same moment Benedicta
was made well, just as if she had never been
afflicted.

Since October, 1753, Bernardin Senagogliese,
a muleteer, had suffered from herpes.   Scratch-
ing aggravated the sores, and the man suffered
much pain.   He was too poor to employ medical aid and was forced by his occupation to
walk much by day and by night, it being impossible for him to ride because of his affliction.
After eight months the ulcers had grown so large
that he could walk only with difficulty and found
it impossible to provide for his family.   A fever
set in, which forced him to take to bed, where for
two days he could find neither sleep nor rest and
was tormented by convulsions and severe pain.
During the night following June 17, 1754, the
pain grew well-nigh unbearable.   Early next

morning the man and his wife implored the aid of Blessed Joseph of Copertino and the wife went to church, further to entreat the saint. Meanwhile the sick man dozed and beheld Blessed Joseph in an apparition. The saint said, "Come, let us recite the Litany of our Lady." Blessed Joseph then began, and the sick man replied to each invocation, "Pray for us." After reciting the words "Health of the Sick," to which Bernardin responded, "Pray for us," the vision vanished, and at the same time all trace of the malady disappeared. The man marvelled much, as did also his wife, who had meanwhile returned from church. Rising at once from his bed and walking with ease to church, Bernardin rendered thanks to God and his benefactor, Blessed Joseph. The rest of the day he spent telling many throughout the city of his recovery. Next morning, being fully restored, he returned to his work.[1]

The feast of St. Joseph was fixed by Pope Benedict XIV in the Brief of Beatification for September 18. The Office and Mass were granted to the Conventuals, Capuchins, Observ-

[1] Positio super miraculis, 1764, pp. 2–3, 13–15, 29.

ants, Reformati, Recollects, Discalced and Third
Order Regular; to the dioceses of Nardo, Assisi,
Fossombrone and Osimo; to Copertino and Pietrarubbia; to the Archconfraternity of St. Antony in Rome and the Confraternity of St.
Stephen in Assisi.[2] On August 8, 1769, Pope
Clement XIV inserted the feast of St. Joseph
into the Roman Missal and Breviary, thereby
extending it to the whole Church.[3]

In 1781, Count John Baptist Sinibaldi erected
a large altar of choice marble in the church of St.
Francis at Osimo, that the remains might be
placed beneath it. Cardinal Guido Calcagnini,
then Bishop of Osimo, after a solemn triduum,
transferred the body to the new high altar on
September 19th of the same year. There it has
remained ever since. The Conventuals remod-
elled the church, which was originally dedicated
to St. Francis, and dedicated it to St. Joseph of
Copertino. Pope Pius VI raised the church to
the dignity of a lesser Basilica.[4]

The sanctuary of St. Joseph of Copertino at

[2] The Brief is given in the first edition of Pastrovicchi
(1753), pp. 97–105.

[3] The Decree is printed in the Bullarium Capucinorum,
vol. IX (Innsbruck, Wagner, 1884), p. 4.

[4] Montanari, 583–585.

INTERIOR OF THE BASILICA OF ST. JOSEPH
OF COPERTINO AT OSIMO

Osimo consists of the chapel in which he said
Mass, and three rooms, one of which served for
receiving persons of rank, while the second was
used by the saint as an oratory and the third
as a living-room and bed-room. Many relics of
St. Joseph are preserved in these rooms. Such
are, clothing worn by him, the chalice and paten,
missal and vestments used by him in saying Mass,
his breviary, devotional books, such as the Imitation of Christ, letters written by him, the picture of our Lady of Grottella presented to him at
Assisi. His oratory is now a chapel [5]

At a meeting of the municipal council of
Osimo, July 26, 1664, the wish was expressed
that Father Joseph be known by the place of his
death as are St. Antony of Padua and St.
Nicholas of Tolentino. The council furthermore
declared the holy friar a citizen of Osimo and
asked that he " implore for the city all bless-
ings." [6] The solemnities in Osimo subsequent
to his canonization gave a new impetus to the cult
of the ecstatic saint and aroused a " holy rivalry
of devotion on the part of the inhabitants and of

[5] Montanari, 580–583; Gattari, 169; St. Franzisci Gloeck-
lein, vol. IV (Innsbruck, Rauch, 1881–1882), pp. 357–358.
[6] Montanari, 546–548.

all manner of benefits on the part of the saint,"
which time has not served to diminish.   One may
well say that in all public and private needs St.
Joseph is the common refuge.   Nor is the devotion restricted to the people of the city.   Many
are the pilgrims who come to Osimo to venerate
the saint and to gaze with mingled reverence and
admiration upon that sacred body to which divine love once gave the power of flight.[7]

[7] Gattari, 168.

INDEX OF NAMES

If you have enjoyed this book, consider making your next selection from among the following . . .

At your Bookdealer or direct from the Publisher.
Toll Free 1-800-437-5876   *Fax 815-226-7770*
Tel. 815-226-7777   *www.tanbooks.com*

Prices subject to change.